STRATEGIC RESUMES
Writing for Results

Marci Mahoney

CRISP PUBLICATIONS, INC.
Menlo Park, California

STRATEGIC RESUMES
Writing for Results

Marci Mahoney

CREDITS:
Editor: **Bev Manber**
Typesetting: **ExecuStaff**
Cover Design: **Kathleen Gadway**
Artwork: **Ralph Mapson**

Copyright © 1992 Marci Mahoney
Printed in the United States of America by Bawden Printing Company.

English language Crisp books are distributed worldwide. Our major international distributors include:

CANADA: Reid Publishing, Ltd., Box 69559—109 Thomas St., Oakville, Ontario Canada L6J 7R4. TEL: (416) 842-4428; FAX: (416) 842-9327

AUSTRALIA: Career Builders, P.O. Box 1051, Springwood, Brisbane, Queensland, Australia 4127. TEL: 841-1061, FAX: 841-1580

NEW ZEALAND: Career Builders, P.O. Box 571, Manurewa, Auckland, New Zealand. TEL: 266-5276, FAX: 266-4152

JAPAN: Phoenix Associates Co., Mizuho Bldg. 2-12-2, Kami Osaki, Shinagawa-Ku, Tokyo 141, Japan. TEL: 3-443-7231, FAX: 3-443-7640

Selected Crisp titles are also available in other languages. Contact International Rights Manager Tim Polk at (800) 442-7477 for more information.

Library of Congress Catalog Card Number 91-76255
Strategic Resumes
Mahoney, Marci
ISBN 1-56052-129-5

This book is printed on recyclable paper with soy ink.

PREFACE

I first became aware of the potential for a resume to be a very special statement 15 years ago. As a Bernard Haldane Associates client, I encountered an approach to resume development that incorporated an objective, summary listing of major skills and series of accomplishments along with the usual sections on education and work.

Using those structural components, my consultant Richard Bell and I came up with a finished product that was a tremendous thrill to me at the time, and the start of a personal fascination with helping other people come up with similarly strong resumes.

I had no written guidelines nor base of samples for reference. The design process initially began on a conceptual level. The core idea seemed to involve building a bridge between past experience and new horizons, of finding links and writing them up persuasively. The resume became a sales tool for developing new work options.

Very gradually, I defined a systematic and detailed methodology for accomplishing that purpose. And while consulting on and editing resumes on the career services staff of a university, came up with the distinguishing feature of this approach—STRATEGIC resumes. The name was a breakthrough perception on what made them distinctive.

Strategy means knowing what you want, and marshalling resources to achieve your goal. It involves stepping outside the regular parameters of thinking about careers, jobs and qualifications. It's an intellectually demanding task that requires practicality and creativity in bringing out your strengths, in building a case for your candidacy.

Special thanks are in order to the many people who have given permission to use their resumes as samples. (To protect privacy, they are all fictionalized). Especially appreciated in this regard are students and alumni of Golden Gate University in San Francisco, and the clients of our firm in Scituate, Massachusetts . . .

And in the production phase of the book, a very grateful acknowledgement to Kent Wampler for his consistent help in refining ideas, streamlining language, and formatting samples. Warm thanks also to Phil Gerould, Publisher at Crisp Publications, Inc., whose sensitivity and facilitative style have been uncommon grace notes in the challenging, slow task of moving this manuscript into print!

DEDICATION

To my husband, Kent F. Wampler, whose insight, supportiveness and companionship light up my life.

To my father, George F. Mahoney, who has been a steady source of stability and perspective in times of personal transition.

To Sr. Gretchen Bogan, valued teacher and cherished friend, whose encouragement to write over the years has helped spark this book.

CONTENTS

ABOUT THIS BOOK

Strategic Resumes offers readers the chance to rethink their personal marketing tool in a series of exercises, resume development strategies, and the eight-step resume production process. Readers have a chance to actively participate in the design and content of their resume with this hands-on workbook. As an additional reward, they experience higher self-esteem as they see their qualifications, strengths and career successes packaged in a strategic, concise and original document sure to make the job applicant stand out and be noticed.

STRATEGIC RESUMES (and the other self-improvement books listed in the back of this book) can be used effectively in a number of ways. Here are some possibilities:

—**Individual Study.** Because the book is self-instructional, all that is needed is a quiet place, some time and a pencil. Completing the activities and exercises, should provide not only valuable feedback, but also practical ideas about steps for self-improvement.

—**Workshops and Seminars.** This book is ideal for pre-assigned reading prior to a workshop or seminar. With the basics in hand, the quality of participation should improve. More time can be spent on concept extensions and applications during the program. The book is also effective when distributed at the beginning of a session.

—**Remote Location Training.** Copies can be sent to those not able to attend ''home office'' training sessions.

—**Informal Study Groups.** Thanks to the format, brevity and low cost, this book is ideal for ''brown-bag'' or other informal group sessions.

There are other possibilities that depend on the objectives of the user. One thing for sure, even after it has been read, this book will serve as excellent reference material which can be easily reviewed. Good luck!

P A R T

1

Change — The New Constant

NEW CHALLENGES IN THE WORK WORLD

We live in a time of dramatic change. It happens fast and continuously alters the shape of the world on every level and in every part of our lives. In particular, today's work world is a challenging arena. From the multinational corporation to the small business sector, change is the new and only constant. Large shifts in the composition of the labor force have occurred. Increased competitive pressures have brought about profound changes in organizations. Traditional definitions of careers no longer apply as new approaches to work design and compensation gain widespread use.

The Challenge of Pathfinding

Conditions in the work world are often hard and uncertain. Very little remains of the old order, of stable organizations and secure careers. The marketplace seems to exist in a state of permanent flux. Routes to opportunity that used to be available have disappeared.

Securing work has become more difficult. Prospects for advancement have diminished. Job security has become elusive. The terms of engagement and formulas for success have become unclear for both organizations and individuals. Loyalty and trust, which traditionally have formed the basis of an implied employment contract, have been replaced by a survival mentality and caution about commitments.

Career paths, in the usual sense, have become casualties of the economic forces. There is no assurance of linear progression through a formal sequence of jobs; organizations are changing, merging and disappearing with disconcerting regularity.

With the landscape of the world of work so changed and continuing to change, our old maps are obsolete. Their information is no longer a reliable indicator for setting a course. Getting from Point A to Point B has become a matter of personal exploration and navigation in uncharted territory.

> PATH-FOLLOWING no longer works . . .
> The task has shifted to PATHFINDING.

The Challenge of Perspective

Perspective is another key to personal career management in the new order. Change can be confusing and hard to manage when there is no "big picture" framework to make sense out of what is happening. Recognizing the broad social forces that are reshaping the workplace can help a lot in developing your own personal gameplan for career success.

TEN TRENDS AFFECTING JOBS

According to *Webster's New Collegiate Dictionary*, a trend is "a prevailing tendency, a general movement, a line of development." How in sync do you feel with the following ten trends? Which do you see as problematic for your job search? Which do you see as beneficial?

New Players

- Baby-boomers, born from the mid-forties to the mid-sixties, have added large numbers of educated workers to the labor force. Initially competing for entry level jobs, they now face increasing competition for decreasing numbers of middle and upper level positions.

- More women have joined the work force, supported by a change in social norms. These women are prepared with high levels of education, motivated by desire for achievement and by economic pressures.

- Immigrants, primarily Hispanic and Asian, have greatly increased the labor force.

A More Highly Educated Work Force

- Over half of all high school graduates continue their education. The number of people in the work force with college degrees has almost doubled in the last 20 years. While emerging jobs require stronger educational credentials, the supply of educated workers is greater than the demand, which frequently leads to underemployment.

Technological Innovation

- Automation and computerization are increasing productivity, while eliminating many unskilled and semiskilled jobs. New professional-level jobs tend to occur in different sectors of the economy and in fewer numbers.

- Improved communications technology is accommodating the use of low-cost technical talent, overseas in decentralized business operations.

A Global Economy

- Decreased demand for goods from labor-intensive industries, continuing trade deficits with foreign nations, and cheaper overseas production costs have led to significant cuts in manufacturing jobs in the United States.

Deregulation

- Governmental withdrawal from the transportation, communication and financial industries has led to price wars and cost-cutting strategies that include layoffs.

Restructurings and Downsizings

- A "do more with less" attitude and changes in the design of jobs that emphasize a self-managing work force, have eliminated many staff and middle-management positions.

- Mergers and acquisitions have led to redundant departments. Many people have become "surplus," prime candidates for redeployment and lay-offs.

Decreasing Strength of Organized Labor

- Unions, as a force in maintaining pay levels and job security, have been weakened. Many unionized jobs have been eliminated because of plant closings and overseas operations, availability of replacement workers, and fewer numbers of unionized workers in growing service sector organizations.

Increasing Use of Temporary Workers

- Companies have reduced the volume of "good jobs," characterized by full-time work, benefits, job security and advancement. Many are turning to two-tier employment systems of core, regular employees and leased, contract employees, and increasing their use of external companies to replace internal departments.

Expanding and Contracting Sectors of Opportunity

- The fast growing and diverse service sector, a small business economy, is the core area for emerging job opportunity. Growth is also happening in the wholesale and retail trade sectors, especially in food stores, bars and restaurants.

- Tax reductions and greater budget pressures have reduced the volume of job opportunity at all levels of government. Manufacturing in "sunset" industries such as steel, auto, tire, textile, apparel and coal is down significantly.

Changing Roles and Reward Systems in Organizations

- A shift away from a formal, sequential progression of jobs is seen in the growth of project-based work that adds value to the enterprise, with pay for performance.

- Expectations of personal decision making and initiative are strong, as is support for growth in skills and knowledge that enhance employability.

Recommended Readings on Changes in the Work World

These are all treasures, solidly researched, with in-depth presentation and thorough analysis:

The Changing Workplace by Carl McDaniels; *The Right Place at the Right Time* by Robert Wegmann and Robert Chapman; *Work in the New Economy, Rev.* by Robert Wegmann, Robert Chapman and Miriam Johnson; *When Giants Learn to Dance* by Rosabeth Moss Kanter; and *Downsizing* by Robert M. Tomasko.

CHANGE-READINESS: AN ADAPTIVE SKILL

The new work place is dynamic and volatile. Uncertainty is certain. Change is inevitable and pervasive. Even in cultures where stability and continuity are prized, external forces influence and sometimes determine business decisions.

On a mega-scale, a shift in oil prices can reverberate through organizations that seem far removed from the energy industry, causing retrenchment through job cuts. Within industries—in transportation, for example—a shake-out among providers can eliminate entire companies. In large organizations, restructuring and downsizing may close whole divisions and departments. In small businesses, survival often depends on trimming jobs to trim overhead.

Apart from what happens "out there," you may notice your own values and interests tugging at you to create change, to open up new horizons. Maybe what you are doing no longer supports your growth. Perhaps you are in an environment that no longer meets your needs. So independently, you are initiating change, inviting it, going after it.

For Surviving and Thriving

Change readiness will be your best friend when you find yourself needing or wanting to make a move. It is a state of mind that is geared to the benefits of new events. It is a resolve to do whatever may be required to achieve a better situation.

When you have change-readiness, you can absorb the pressures of disruptive or displacing outside factors. You can move ahead with your life. When you have change-readiness, you are attuned to your instincts around what you need to do to earn a living and you can create your right livelihood.

Catalysts for change can be external or internal. For the change-ready person, it does not matter. What matters is his or her core disposition to relate to change, to see it as a vehicle for important personal and career development.

On Developing Change-Readiness

Developing change-readiness may mean doing some emotional homework. It may mean recognizing the pull of the familiar, of the status quo, and getting in touch with your motivation for a more meaningful alternative. It may mean developing a shield against wavering thoughts about your personal potential and outside influences that discourage your move.

You may want to look at your support systems, the people in your life who believe in you and want you to succeed. These are the people who will listen to you, talk with you frankly, cheer you on, and in various other ways be invaluable resources.

Finally, you may want to take a look at what you can do to build in flexibility for taking quick and effective action in new career initiatives. How clear are you about realistic and attractive options? How prepared are you to discuss opportunities with new employers?

"CHANGE-READINESS QUIZ"

A CHANGE-READINESS QUIZ

Place a check on the scale below for each of the following statements, at the point that best describes how you relate to change:

1. I find change to be basically:

   Disruptive ———————————————————————— **Stimulating**

2. I see change as:

   Crisis ——————————————————————————— **Opportunity**

3. I make changes:

   When necessary ————————————————————— **When possible**

4. I handle change:

   With difficulty —————————————————————— **With ease**

Circle the response that describes your current career situation:

5. I have a "Plan A" for my next career move.   **Yes**   **No**

6. I have a "Plan B" for my next career move.   **Yes**   **No**

7. I have at least three months of income saved   **Yes**   **No**
   as a buffer against unemployment.

8. I have some realistic ideas about interim jobs   **Yes**   **No**
   I could do, if I need to.

Complete the following unfinished sentences:

• A change I want to make in my employment situation is:

   _____

• Factors I have going for me in making this change include:

   _____

• Additional things I can do to enhance my change-readiness are:

   _____

MANAGING CHANGE BY MANAGING YOUR CAREER

In the midst of changing workplace conditions, there is a resource for path-finding—a very powerful and reliable resource. It is a way for you to find direction when there are no external signs and signals telling you where to go and when to stop and go. It is the bridge to opportunity when the old roads are no longer serviceable.

Career Management:
A Concept, a Set of Skills and a Personal Commitment

► The Career Management Concept

The core concept in career management is that you have the freedom and the responsibility to manage your own career. No one else can do it for you. No one else will do it for you. And no one else will care as much about your career.

When managing your career becomes a self-directed process, you gain a great deal of control over your working life. You take ownership of realizing your personal potential. You become a stakeholder in developing ways to earn a living, no matter what options close down for you along the way.

When you claim the career management concept as your own personal outlook, you gain a stabilizing perspective for handling the toughest of transitions. *And* you become energized to create work that you really want to do, work that you will value and enjoy, work that will be a source of meaning and vitality, contribution and growth.

► Career Management Skills

Career management is based on several very important skills—abilities for you to develop, use and refine at every stage of your working life.

Career management means identifying what you have to offer and what you want to do. It means defining goals that are consistent with your greatest strengths and interests, connected to needs in the marketplace. It means scouting out opportunity that is often in obscure and unexpected places, and communicating effectively with people who can help leverage you for a position or hire you.

CAREER MANAGEMENT (continued)

Once selected for a new job or a new assignment, career management means delivering peak performance, staying attuned constantly to adding value, practicing learning as a way of life, and building and maintaining strong relationships with your co-workers, colleagues and customers.

► Career Management Commitment

Your commitment to managing your career will be the single most important factor in your success. It will get you going and keep you going when times are hard. It will help you to take horizon-broadening risks. It will drive every initiative you make, and motivate employers to invest in themselves by investing in you.

P A R T

2

Resumes
in Perspective

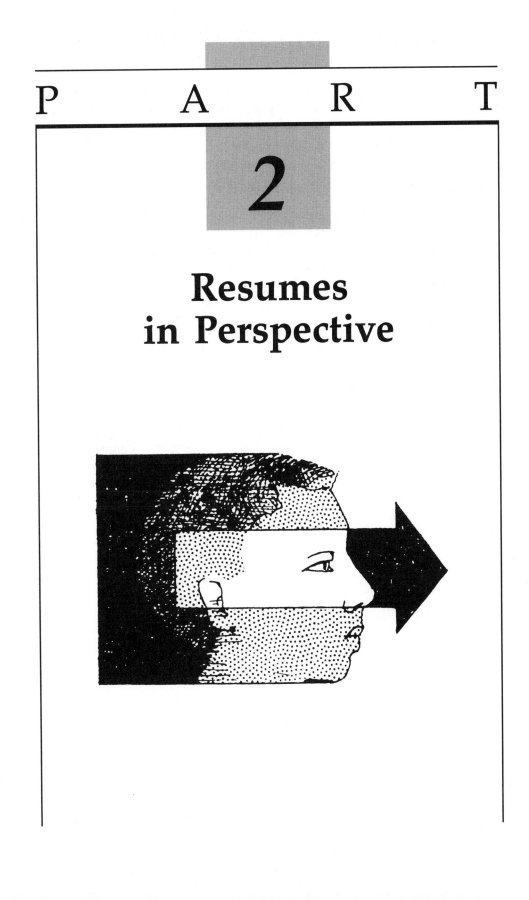

A POSITIONING STEP

Having your resume at hand is an important positioning step for attaining new employment. With it, you know you can quickly respond to an attractive job opportunity. Your resume gives employers a clear message that you are interested in being considered for a position.

Your resume is a factual document about your history. It symbolizes your interest in new horizons. Your decision to write your resume is a commitment to your career management. It shows you are becoming change-ready in a very practical and important way.

A Job Search Ritual

A resume is a ceremonial job search practice, widely expected and used. It is a traditional tool in hiring and job seeking, and plays a key role in communications between employers and applicants.

A resume may be a powerful conveyor of meaning, or serve as a routine formality. By developing a strategic resume, you make a vital and valuable statement about yourself, and gain a very effective resource.

Contrary to popular belief, resumes do not have to be written only one way. As long as you are honest about yourself, you have tremendous freedom to be creative.

Resume Myth-Busting

You may have some unlearning to do as you think about your new resume. A whole series of limiting notions has grown up around resumes. If you find yourself believing that a resume should be written only one way, think again.

Your resume is not a job application form, with a standardized set of information. It is a highly individualized statement of your work interests and related assets. Let go of attachments you have to ideas about content and format, categories and sequence, and see what emerges. Consider the following:

- An effective resume is a sales tool, not an autobiography.
- A descriptive resume is easy to write; a persuasive resume is what works.
- Draw material for your resume from any area of your life.
- Emphasize experiences that best support your objective.
- Influence the way others see you by the way you see and describe yourself.

A PART OF A LARGER JOB SEARCH PROCESS

There is a widespread belief that a great resume will get you a great job. They are sure that outstanding construction, creative presentation of content and beautiful graphics will make you an irresistible candidate—doors will automatically open, and opportunity will knock. This is wishful thinking.

In fact, a great many variables affect who gets what opportunities where, when and how. Some variables fall within your control, such as the strength of your resume, your job search method, and your commitment to results. Other variables fall outside of your control, like a politicized hiring process or selection criteria that change.

At best, a resume is a paper statement to use in your job search. It has no magical properties, even when it is captivating. And it may be subject to the biases of its readers, even when it is not in their best interest to discount it.

> ## A Job Search Paradox:
>
> *Do not under-estimate or over-estimate the importance of your resume.*

Your resume is worth a great deal of thought. It can reflect you at your best, and be a key aid in your job search communications. It can help you to build a clear and convincing case for your candidacy and to stand out from other applicants.

While a strong resume can influence your job search, hiring decisions are made on the basis of *personal* contact. Employers may be receptive to you because of your resume; they will decide about hiring you on the basis of their direct experience with you.

A Means to an End, Not an End in Itself

So, in working on your resume, give it your best. Think about every detail of its design. Aim to make it a core ingredient in your job search success.

Then look at what *else* you can do in your job search activities. What can you do more, less, or differently to achieve results? What do marketplace conditions demand of you? What is the best use of your time? How many outreaches can you make this week? How much follow-up can you do with people you have written, called or seen?

The secret of a successful job search is in maintaining a positive attitude. You need to do *everything* humanly possible to build in success, and faithfully and persistently keep at it until you get your breakthrough, find your niche, start your job.

AN EXERCISE IN PERSONAL GROWTH

When you move beyond a basic summary of background information probing into what makes you special, writing your resume can be a very powerful exercise in personal growth.

A Source of Insight

Defining the focus of your resume requires careful thought. Consider what you would really like to do, what you think you can do, and how much you want to do it. Your focus will include issues of

- **Meaning**—How satisfying is the work that you have been doing? Does it make sense to maintain your current career focus?

- **Purpose**—What do you want to do in your next job? What kind of career involvement draws you and excites you?

- **Risk-taking**—How big a change would you like to make, if any? How comfortable do you feel in following your heart?

A Source of Self-Esteem

Get set for a thoroughly enjoyable side-effect of resume writing. Identifying your personal qualities and attitudes that support your effectiveness is highly pleasurable and a tremendous source of self-esteem. While it may take some effort to focus in on your most important assets, you are likely to enjoy what you discover and feel very proud of yourself.

Thinking about what you do best, defining the ways in which you make a difference, in which you have an impact, recalling examples of excellent performance, of personal contribution . . . this is a good prescription for rainy days, not just resume development!

Describing your strengths helps build and strengthen a positive self-concept. This serves as a reminder of your capabilities and potential during hard times in your career. And it helps you to feel and project confidence when an employer asks the predictable questions: ''Why are you here?'' ''What can you do for me?'' and ''Why should I hire you?''

REFLECTIONS ON RESUMES

Take a few moments to think through each of these questions before answering.

1. A resume is important to me at this time because . . .

2. I need a ready-to-use resume by . . .

3. In today's job market, a strong resume is . . .

4. I am interested in a new approach to writing a resume because . . .

5. Resumes I have seen in the past . . .

6. I used to think that a resume should . . .

7. My opinion of traditional resumes is . . .

8. The hardest part about writing a resume is . . .

9. The most rewarding part of writing a resume is . . .

10. The best way for me to produce a resume will be to . . .

P A R T

3

Strategic Resumes
for Competitive Edge

A MATTER OF STANDARDS

As you prepare your resume, you need to make a very important decision about standards. On the most basic level, you can state what you have done and where you have been—a very plain and simple option. On the highest level, you can craft a statement about yourself that is an art form in personal communication.

How important is it to you to produce the very best possible statement about yourself and why you should be hired? How important is it to you to go all out to convince a prospective employer that you are a valuable potential resource?

The Basic Approach

If your chief concern in resume-writing is sketching an outline of your background, your task will be quick and easy. It takes very little effort to list the basic facts of your education and employment. No one could fault you on such a presentation. You could reply to ads and other listings of job openings. You would be safely in compliance with requests for a personal resume.

An all-purpose statement about your history would be simple and straightforward to write. You could use it with any prospective employer and know that you have provided all the information necessary to be assessed for a position.

This basic approach has one small problem. It does not distinguish you and set you apart from other job-seekers. While you conform to basic job search protocol, you gain no competitive advantage in gaining an appealing new position.

Unless the core facts of your education and your employment are awesomely impressive in their own right, and relate exactly and extensively to a particular hiring need, the basic approach is of limited value. In some cases, it may even weaken your candidacy for employment.

A MATTER OF STANDARDS (continued)

The Give-It-All-You-Have Approach

If your chief concern in resume writing is doing everything you can on your resume to motivate an employer to take an interest in you, this approach will be for you. You will have to invest a considerable amount of time and effort. You will have to think hard about the work you want to do and your qualifications for that work. It will take discipline and patience to achieve a quality end result.

This is a targeted approach. You will define and declare your focus, and then support it in every way possible in the rest of your resume. You will consider your selling points from every angle and identify what is most important to bring out about yourself.

It may mean drafting and redrafting. It may mean deleting some details that you have assumed are ''givens'' to present about yourself. It may mean identifying and adding information about yourself that you have not previously considered.

This give-it-all-you-have approach is built on a creative and venturesome way of thinking about yourself and your career that may fundamentally alter the form of your resume, and fundamentally increase the chances of your job search success.

THE POWER OF STRATEGY

A strategy is:

- a careful plan or method that affords the maximum support
- the art of devising plans toward a goal to meet under advantageous conditions
- of great importance within an integrated whole.

Let's look at the benefits of strategy in resume development. Assume that a resume can open doors to discussions about employment or can remind you and prospective employers of your ability to contribute.

Much Is at Stake

On a strictly financial level, landing a new job may provide you many thousands of dollars in additional income. On a professional level, you may be ready and restless for new challenge and opportunity. And on a personal level, you may be up for a breakthrough that deepens or restores your sense of well-being in the world of work.

You have a limited amount of space—two pages at the most—to present yourself to an employer. You have a limited amount of time to make your point. You may have other circumstances that negatively affect how you are perceived. Even in the best of circumstances, you may have serious competition for the same desirable jobs.

So, you have a lot to gain from a strategic approach to your resume. A strategic resume offers you a means to stand out in your job search, moving beyond the routine scope of your vital statistics to provide convincing support for you being hired.

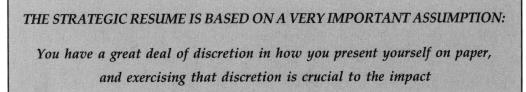

THE STRATEGIC RESUME IS BASED ON A VERY IMPORTANT ASSUMPTION:

You have a great deal of discretion in how you present yourself on paper, and exercising that discretion is crucial to the impact your resume will have in the job market.

THE STRATEGIC APPROACH

When you think strategically about your career initiatives, you look carefully at what you want to attain, assess assets that could help you and liabilities that could hinder you, and develop a game plan for successfully utilizing the unique factors of your situation.

Using this process, you take control of your career and affirm the value of your abilities and experiences. You commit yourself to establishing a persuasive case why you should be hired for the work you want to do.

Relating to Hiring Concerns

Building on a clearly defined area of career focus, you develop perspective on the hiring concerns of employers in that area of work. You learn problems that face them and the results they want to achieve. You consider your career aspirations through the eyes of employers, assess what they may value about you, and write your resume accordingly.

You position yourself as a contributor, one who can relate to an employer's needs and objectives, make a difference and add value. You delineate a history of direct or related experience that demonstrates you can do the job and do it well, at whatever level of responsibility is realistic.

You define your personal attributes, themes in your experience, and the applicable accomplishments that make you a serious candidate and a desirable recruit. You motivate the employer to want to talk with you.

Creative Judgment Calls

Through a series of creative judgment calls on the *selection, phrasing, sequencing* and *depth of treatment* of the facts of your background, you develop a powerful written sales tool to support your candidacy. Your resume reflects you at your best, structures perception accordingly, and paves the way to opportunities for you to grow and thrive in work.

Truth in Advertising

A non-negotiable aspect of strategic resume writing is that every statement that you make is true, and you give a full and fair picture of your background as it relates to your objective.

On a very serious level, the resume is a legal document used in selection decisions. The reliability of all information on it is a condition of any subsequent employment. Statements you make form the basis of a good faith relationship with a new employer, and give a blueprint of how you can be used most effectively.

So, a strategic resume is an authentic expression of who you are and what you offer. Writing it is *also* a creative exercise in bringing forth and emphasizing your most relevant personal assets.

PERSUASIVE CASE-BUILDING

What information would an employer most appreciate knowing about you, and would establish your ability as a contributor? What attitudes do you have that suit you to the work you would like to do? Which of your life experiences are most relevant to describe? What skills and accomplishments would be most useful to highlight?

> ## A Job Search Paradox:
>
> All *of your experience counts;* some *of your experience applies.*

When you write your strategic resume, you look at the full range of your life experience as potential source material. In assessing items for inclusion, there are no artificial distinctions made between paid and unpaid experiences, recent and more distant experiences. Experience is experience.

Your greatest achievement may have been the volunteer work you did for the United Way. An extracurricular school activity may be the basis of many important activities which recommend you for employment. A project on your job which falls outside your regular responsibilities may be the most striking indicator of your interests and abilities. A special accomplishment in an earlier job may date back in time, but be well worth citing.

At the same time, the principle of selectivity applies. Why is a particular personal quality or experience important to cite on your resume? How does it strengthen your candidacy? Is it a miscellaneous detail taking up space, or is it a vital part of persuasive case-building?

A Shift in Time Orientation from the Past to the Future

Evaluating what to include in your resume becomes much easier when you shift from a focus from past to future. All sorts of information recedes in importance when you ask, ''Is this relevant to what I now want to do?'' This question becomes a filter for distinguishing between important and unimportant experiences.

A key flaw in conventional resumes is preoccupation with the past. They emphasize employment history, giving unabridged descriptions of more than any employer wants to know or could digest.

On the other hand, strategic resumes look to the future. They are focused, uncluttered statements of interest and ability. They are streamlined profiles of your most pertinent strengths. They are tailored messages to targeted audiences. They are bridges between what you have done and what you want to do, and are the key to new and rewarding careers.

CASE-BUILDING CAMEO

CASE-BUILDING CAMEO

Claire is a mother of two young sons. She is interested in a job at her children's school or at another local school. Prior to becoming a homemaker, she had a long history in the travel industry, where she held numerous positions in travel agencies and with an airlines.

Designing her strategic resume, Claire has several options for positioning herself in her new area of interest:

Within her Objective: She can identify Early Childhood School Services including Toddlers, Preschool and Lower Elementary School Children, and flag four potential roles she could play: Childcare; Classroom Assisting; Volunteer Coordination; and Administrative Support.

Within her Summary of Qualifications: She can cite her parent-teacher association activities, hands-on familiarity with children's educational toys and books, extensive business background utilizing interpersonal and organizational skills, and personal qualities that particularly suit her to work with children: being attentive, receptive, patient, calm and adaptive.

Within her Key Skills and Related Experience Section: She can define her applicable functional-transferable skills (observing; listening; encouraging; facilitating and planning; organizing; coordinating; and problem-solving). She can give specific examples from her extensive parent involvement and volunteer activities, which emphasize the informal knowledge base and motivation she has to take on a paid school job.

Within her Employment Section: She can reference her job titles, affiliations, locations and dates, without further elaboration.

Within her Education Section: She can list her bachelor's degree, college and location, and identify her major in Travel and Tourism in an optional citation.

A conventional resume for Claire would have no obvious links between her formal qualifications and the work she now wants to do. A job-by-job description of her employment history would not interest a school principal. Claire's numerous skills, personal qualities and informal qualifications would be omitted, which are of crucial relevance to her new job objective.

NOTE:

While Claire's story is a dramatic example of career change, the strategic resume also benefits people continuing to follow their current lines of work, at all levels of responsibility, and in all kinds of specialized roles and industries.

You begin with the uniqueness of your personal situation, building the best possible case for being hired that the facts of your experience allow.

Category headings, sequencing of categories, decisions on what to bring forth and elaborate on, and what to condense and de-emphasize, all creative judgment calls you will make as you develop your strategic resume.

4

The Eight-Step Formula

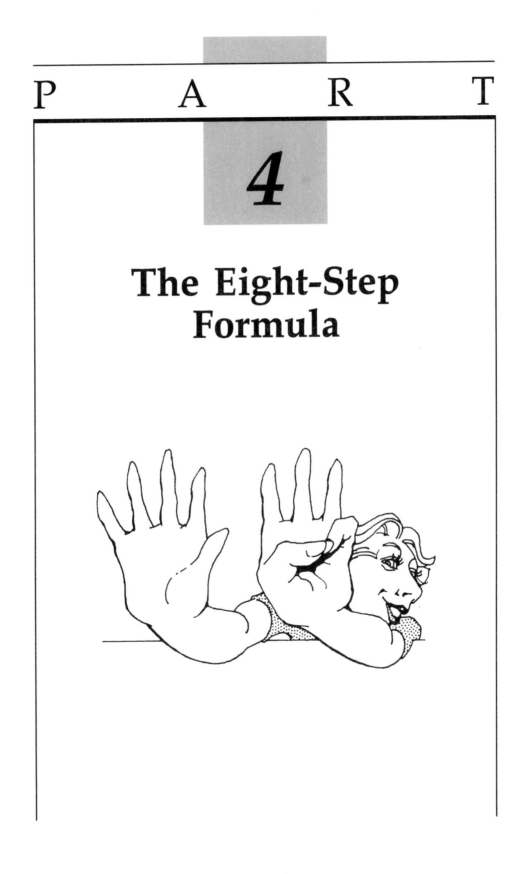

STRATEGIC RESUME PRODUCTION

Producing a strategic resume takes commitment. It means devoting the time to each step to achieve a strong end result. You can quickly generate a resume if circumstances require, but need to deal with each step even as you expedite completion. There are no shortcuts in the process, only intensification of effort. Quality comes from attention to every detail, from start to finish.

You may find it useful to review *The Eight-Step Formula* and the sample resumes before beginning work on your own resume. Getting the "big picture" of the production process will give you a sense of the purpose of each of the steps and how they all fit together. Noting issues and techniques of special relevance to your situation will make it easier to think strategically about the handling of your own experience.

Your resume is a highly personal and important document. It should clearly support your objective, reflect what makes you special in language you are comfortable using, and have graphics that are thoroughly professional. The strategic resume production process makes the most of what you have to offer for the work you want to do.

THE EIGHT-STEP FORMULA

STEP 1: DEFINE YOUR OBJECTIVE

STEP 2: ASSESS YOUR MARKETABILITY

STEP 3: SELECT YOUR FORMAT

STEP 4: BUILD YOUR BASE

STEP 5: DEVELOP A DRAFT

STEP 6: REFINE THE QUALITY

STEP 7: PACKAGE WITH CARE

STEP 8: RUN A QUALITY CHECK

STEP 1: DEFINE YOUR OBJECTIVE

Defining your objective is at the heart of developing a strategic resume. By zeroing in on what you want, you can feature the most *relevant* aspects of who you are and what you have done. You are creating a guide that will help you decide what to say about yourself, which will build your case for work opportunities you are best suited to, and most desire.

On Staying "Open"

You may say, "Ah, but what if defining an objective on my resume eliminates me from being considered for a job I might not have thought of, but am qualified to do?" or "I want to keep my options OPEN—open to anything that can be a source of income and stability, a toehold in an organization of interest."

Reciting your personal background for employers to evaluate will not catch the attention of an employer with very specific hiring needs, thus reducing your chances for becoming an applicant. Defining your objective will help you be noticed.

The Distinction of Personal Focus

On the average, resumes get a 30 second review. If your objective, what your contributing role can be, what area of the organization you are oriented to are unclear, you will probably never talk with a person with the power to hire or recommend your hiring.

Your challenge is to stand out immediately and impressively as an attractive candidate for employment. A focused, targeted resume can make a highly positive first impression of you as a career-minded person, clear about your professional interests and persuasive about your related strengths.

An Inner-Directed Approach to Your Job Search

This approach means laying aside impulsive response to job possibilities "out there," especially when they are a variety of unlikely openings listed in the weekly classifieds. It requires that you develop an inner compass to the kinds of work most likely to give you satisfaction and success, with faith in your inherent marketability while you pursue what you do best and most enjoy.

STEP 1: DEFINE YOUR OBJECTIVE (continued)

Identifying an objective reflects a job search philosophy that states the benefits of focus are greater than the risks. You have much more to gain by targeting your resume toward acquiring a specific kind of work.

And if you find more than one career option that you would like to explore, the principle of focus still holds true: state an objective for each option, reflecting your interest and strengths. Tailor your resume accordingly.

A Job Search Paradox:

The more focused you are, the greater your career opportunities will tend to be.

Consider how this works from the employer's point of view. Pause for a moment and place yourself in the shoes of a key manager experiencing a particular unmet or undermet need—the basis of all hiring.

Imagine you own a small business. Something is holding you back from solving a problem, implementing a key strategy, or increasing your market share. You have hard-won and limited resources you want to maximize, and have identified a particular staffing requirement as vital to moving ahead.

As this employer, you review a file of resumes maintained by the personnel department. What speaks to you most—a general background profile without an objective or a focused resume, targeted to your areas of concern and including related skills and accomplishments?

Which resumes impress you and catch your attention as you grapple with ongoing business challenges and varied demands on your time? Which people do you feel have stronger interests in and commitments to contributing in the area you need coverage for—those with or without an objective?

What have you learned or confirmed from this perspective?

A QUICK QUIZ

1. How clear is your focus on your professional identity?

2. What kind of work do you want to be doing in your next job?

3. Briefly describe your job objective.

A Resume Objective—Some Definitions

▶ A statement that specifies your preferred kind of work

▶ A description of the contributing role you wish to play, or the function you seek involvement in your next job

▶ Your short-term employment focus, supported by personal interests and skills

▶ A realistic aspiration, emerging from your demonstrable experience base

NOTE: Your objective is distinct from your ideal job, visions, dreams, and fantasies of career satisfaction—which may guide your thinking about occupational direction—but not be sources of your personal livelihood.

Achievable and Motivating

Notice the basic practicality of a resume objective. It should stand up well under scrutiny and probing. You should be able to accomplish it.

If you are entering a line of work that your education directly qualifies you for, or seeking a new opportunity based on your prior job experiences, defining your resume objective will be fairly straightforward.

On the other hand, if you are seeking work with meaning for the first time, or are changing careers into distinctly new and different work, then defining your resume objective in even generically descriptive terms may be a challenge.

GUIDELINES FOR YOUR OBJECTIVE

Here are a few guidelines for developing your resume objective. Complete the exercise that follows each guideline. (Ideally, you would want to participate in a formal career assessment and planning process.)

Guideline #1: First and foremost, *trust your instincts.*

What do they tell you about the kind of work you are suited to do that will build upon your most notable strengths and interests?

I see myself doing, working at, dedicated to, excelling in _____

_____

_____

_____

_____

Guideline #2: Define *variations on a theme.*

What kind of jobs lie outside of your direct work experience, but are indirectly related, are of an allied nature, share some common skill/knowledge base?

_____

_____

_____

_____

Guideline #3: Think about work in terms of *products and services.*

Which products and services intrigue you, delight you, inspire you or otherwise draw you to them?

Products of interest _____

Related jobs I might do _____

Services of interest _____

Related jobs I might do _____

Guideline #4: Use your *imagination,* tempered by *self-awareness.*

Imagine that a special make-a-wish foundation will underwrite you pursuing what you would most like to do for work. The only condition is that it must build solidly on a dimension of your experience that will support your occupations. Write your job description.

_____

_____

_____

_____

Guideline #5: What *insights* can you gain from your *significant others*?

What do key people in your personal life see as realistic and compatible work for you, that builds upon your talents and enthusiasms?

_____

_____

_____

_____

Upon consideration, I would most like the key thrust of my job objective to emphasize:

_____

_____

_____

_____

_____

_____

_____

_____

_____

STEP 2: ASSESS YOUR MARKETABILITY

Your next step in developing a strategic resume is to carefully assess your marketability. Your task is to examine thoroughly the major pluses and minuses of your candidacy for the work you want. This process will help you identify your special selling points and assist you in handling areas of complexity.

Your Marketability

Assuming your job objective is based upon a significant interest and strength, and there is a need or demand for what you want to do, YOU ARE MARKETABLE.

You are a valuable potential employment resource in the world of work, defined as the exchange of skilled service for money and other benefits. For work in your target area, chosen after considerable reflection on its suitability for you, you have much to give. Your personal qualities make you an asset. Your experiences demonstrate your effectiveness.

Your task in marketing yourself is to communicate with exquisite clarity the particular ways you can excel and contribute, with employers who have a need that you can meet. Your mandate—and your opportunity—is to build a compelling case for being hired, to demonstrate vividly why it is in an employer's enlightened self-interest to bring you on board.

Some Myths About Marketability

Some might have you believe that to be marketable you must be perfect. They claim you must match all specifications for a position, that no departure from an idealized profile will be tolerated, that you must conform in all respects to conventional definitions of "qualified."

Similar beliefs are that you should be neither too young nor too old, neither overqualified nor underqualified, and have no deficits in formal education, no gaps in your employment history, and no irregularities in who you are, what you look like, and what you have done with your life.

Furthermore, the party line of doomsdayers and naysayers holds that in difficult economic times it is too competitive to try anything you have not done before. They are convinced that going after work that you would enjoy is not practical or feasible, and is a waste of time.

Finally, your gloomy advisors may sign off with admonitions about the importance of presenting yourself to employers in proper, standard ways—particularly on your resume. They may advise you to use an extremely familiar format, outlining the chronology of your background. They may be sure that this will enable employers to best exercise their expert judgment on your appropriateness for a job.

Taking Back Control

If you have found yourself buying into such beliefs, it is time to take back control. Before you can write a strategic resume and use it effectively, you need to become an iconoclast—''one who attacks established beliefs''—whenever commonly circulating ideas diminish your hope and limit your horizons.

Your ability to influence employers' perceptions of you will begin with your perceptions of your own value, and your firm commitment to demonstrate that value creatively and convincingly. You may need to push the limits of your own assumptions about qualifications, in thinking about which of your assets recommend you for employment.

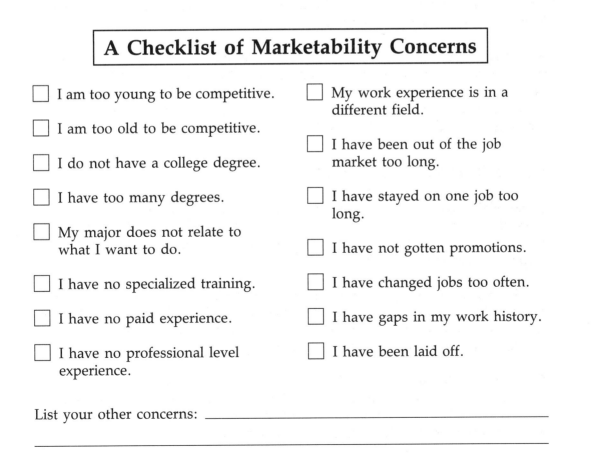

A Checklist of Marketability Concerns

☐ I am too young to be competitive.

☐ I am too old to be competitive.

☐ I do not have a college degree.

☐ I have too many degrees.

☐ My major does not relate to what I want to do.

☐ I have no specialized training.

☐ I have no paid experience.

☐ I have no professional level experience.

☐ My work experience is in a different field.

☐ I have been out of the job market too long.

☐ I have stayed on one job too long.

☐ I have not gotten promotions.

☐ I have changed jobs too often.

☐ I have gaps in my work history.

☐ I have been laid off.

List your other concerns: _____

_____

STEP 2: MARKETABILITY (continued)

Marketability Concerns as Strategic Challenges

As you review your concerns about your marketability, keep this crucial point in mind: no aspect of your history or circumstances has the power to block you from your goals. This is a key operating assumption for writing a strategic resume *and* for managing your career!

In other words, you are in the driver's seat of how you look at your situation and influence others to look at it. When you really set your mind to it, you can determine, to an extraordinarily large degree, how you are perceived and evaluated.

It is practically a given that somewhere, somehow, something will pose a problem in job search communications. While complicating factors are likely to come up, how you deal with them is very much a matter of choice.

You may have one or more areas of potential complexity to address. You may need to give special attention and careful handling to how you present some fact or facts about yourself. You may have work to do on reassessing your beliefs and habitual ways of looking at matters that set you apart from a classically qualified candidate.

The idea is to remain in charge of your self-presentation, to be matter-of-fact in handling objections, and resourceful and positive in refocusing attention on your skills and related accomplishments.

Your confidence and strength in the job market will be directly proportionate to your ability to take your marketability concerns and treat them as strategic challenges.

Examples:

- If you are concerned about your age, you can de-emphasize or delete dates and bring out the strengths of your substantial experience.

- If you do not have a college degree, you can emphasize the strength of your job experience and employer-sponsored training.

- If your work experience is in a different field, you can focus on the transferability of your skills and any avocational bridges to your new line of work.

The Skill of Reframing

Whenever you recast your situation, you use the skill of reframing. This is the art of stepping outside the ordinary, automatic ways of looking at situations, and bringing up new and important dimensions that are worthy of attention.

In strategic resume development, making the most of the facts and helping others to see your hidden strengths is *a key resource.*

A QUICK PERSONAL ASSESSMENT

Answering the following questions will help clarify your beliefs about your job search prospects.

1. The most challenging part of achieving my job objective will be:

2. The marketability myth I am most vulnerable to believing is:

3. The most predictable objection to hiring me is likely to be:

4. A particular concern I have in presenting my qualifications is:

5. A strategy that may be very useful to winning receptivity is to:

6. A belief that I am reevaluating about job search technique is that:

7. I see the impact of the economy on my job prospects as:

8. My commitment to getting work in the area of my job objective is:

GAMEPLAN FOR SUCCESS

RESUME OBJECTIVE: Short-term employment goal

_____

_____

_____

_____

_____

MARKETABILITY PLUSES: Significant strengths, special selling points

_____

_____

_____

_____

_____

MARKETABILITY MINUSES: Possible or predictable obstacles and objections

_____

_____

_____

_____

_____

PERSONAL RESUME STRATEGY: Ideas for linking what I have done to what I want to do

_____

_____

_____

_____

_____

STEP 3: SELECT YOUR FORMAT

Selecting your resume format is a major strategic decision. Real and compelling differences characterize the two most common formats, which have impact on the receptivity employers have to your initiatives.

No universally "right" format is appropriate for all people. Your review of your own objective and background will be your most effective guide to selecting the best format for you.

THE CHRONOLOGICAL FORMAT

Your employment record is the primary organizing principle for this format, a job-by-job historical narrative of your work effectiveness.

Merits:

- This format accentuates your formal qualifications for the work you are seeking. Appropriate for directly qualified candidates with linear progression paths, it showcases the track record of clearly pertinent, often increasingly responsible experiences. Seasoned judgment in grappling with job challenges is emphasized.

- Recruiters and some hiring managers are accustomed to, and often prefer, a traditional format. Many find it familiar, straightforward and easy to use when making preliminary decisions of inclusion and exclusion.

Drawbacks:

- For candidates who are starting or changing a career, this format emphasizes the lack of direct, in-depth experience in the targeted career area. It underscores past identity rather than future potential.

- Gaps in employment, conspicuously brief or long affiliations, and time periods elapsed since certain qualifying experiences are spotlighted.

- Rather than accenting accomplishments on and off the job, it lends itself to a somewhat dry, repetitive recitation of job responsibilities.

Criteria for Use:

The chronological format is particularly effective for people with clearcut qualifications, who are continuing or advancing in a particular career direction. It is acceptable for other, less overtly qualified people. This format can be productive if you cite relevant skills and tasks that support your objective within the job-by-job description.

STEP 3: SELECT YOUR FORMAT (continued)

THE FUNCTIONAL FORMAT

Your key skills, knowledge and related accomplishments are the primary organizing principles of this format, citing relevant examples of effectiveness as proof and prediction of your ability to contribute.

Merits:

- This format provides an opportunity to establish the transferability of skills and accomplishments for candidates who are starting or changing a career. Grouping these items in self-contained categories builds a case for your ability to function in a new situation. The conventional resume format dilutes or contradicts this talent.

- Not limited to paid employment, you can give status to qualifying experience from every area of life. This format widens the scope of informal experiences supportive of your career objective, including special projects, internships, community service and relevant leisure pursuits. It eliminates distinctions that discount their importance.

Drawbacks:

- For directly qualified candidates with a linear progression path, this format challenges the standard presentation of personal strengths. Executive recruiters and other employment professionals prefer a job-by-job description to trace with clarity exactly what has been done, for whom, where and when.

- Some employers assume that this format hides background information of importance.

- In a purely functional resume, key time/space anchors that employers expect are not given. This information can be essential to credibility.

Criteria for Use:

- The functional format is particularly effective and highly recommended for people without direct experience in the area of their career objective. Since it accents skills and achievements, it is effective and often desired by people who are well established in a career.

THE COMBINATION FORMAT

The combination format recognizes the inherent drawbacks of both the chronological and functional formats used in their pure forms.

► The pure chronological resume is too mundane, a bland work autobiography. It is descriptive, but tends not to be persuasive about personal qualifications.

► The pure functional resume is too free-floating and reads like a set of assertions about abilities, unlinked to verifiable sources of confirmation.

► Whether you prefer the chronological or functional format, the most effective resume blends the best elements of each.

The Chronological-Combination Resume:

This format retains the structure of a job-by-job delineation of experience and emphasizes accomplishments, the hallmark of the functional resume.

The Functional-Combination Resume:

This format retains the structure of key skills, knowledges and accomplishments, incorporating a distilled EXPERIENCE section, which denotes career-related time/space anchors, the hallmark of the chronological resume.

All References to Resumes in This Guide Assume a Combination Format:

Chronological-combination resumes and functional-combination resumes will be referred to simply as chronological and functional resumes.

STEP 4: BUILD YOUR BASE

Develop a thorough data base of your potentially qualifying experiences. This ensures that you consider all possible factors that support your career objective. Care with this step gives you a rich foundation to draw on as you write your draft. This enables you to write a quality resume as quickly as possible. For greater flexibility use separate sheets of paper to make your lists.

✔ Review Your Learning Experiences

List the particulars of each academic program in your educational background:

- High school diploma, name of school, location, year of completion
- Name and location of each college or university attended, number of credits earned, focus of studies, degree, year of completion
- Merit scholarships, coursework relevant to your objective, research studies, theses, projects, internships, student leadership activities

List all career-related seminars you have taken, including noncredit workshops both in the community and on the job:

- Professional development seminars, sponsor and depth/duration
- Certificate programs

✔ Review Your Work Experiences

Trace your employment record and other qualifying experiences such as community service:

- Title, organization, location, dates
- Responsibilities
- Accomplishments

✔ Review Your Leisure Experiences

List your leisure pursuits, both present and past:

- Avocations
- Applicable skills and knowledges
- Accomplishments

STEP 5: DEVELOP YOUR DRAFT

As you begin to develop your draft, remember that it is your first effort. It does not need to be marvelous. The challenge in the drafting phase is to generate thinking and phrasing that can be improved as needed.

Writer's block generally reflects an intimidating concern with perfection that makes it nearly impossible to write. Treat your draft as a preliminary exercise, an experiment in wordsmithing, and see what you get.

When you give yourself permission to take this approach to your draft, you will find that while the process takes thought and concentration, it is surprisingly manageable. The pressure for premature results is off.

Reserve a block of time that will be sufficient to write a good first draft—preferably a full morning, afternoon or evening. Remove distractions and interruptions. Get as comfortable as you can. Have your reference materials handy.

Reread this *Strategic Resumes* guide. Reflect on what you want to bring out about yourself, jotting notes as you go. Take a deep breath, and step-by-step, write your draft.

Aim to write one or two pages. The length will depend upon your personal preference, and the scope and depth of your experience that supports your objective. Be relevant, clear and specific.

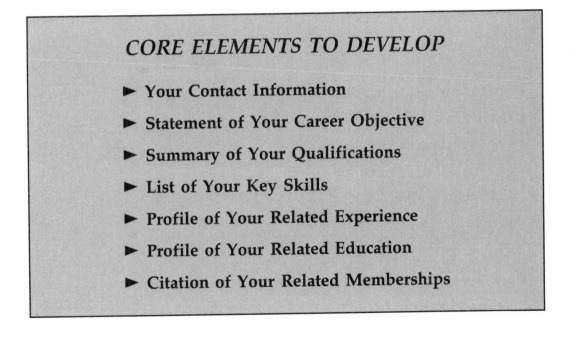

CORE ELEMENTS TO DEVELOP

► **Your Contact Information**

► **Statement of Your Career Objective**

► **Summary of Your Qualifications**

► **List of Your Key Skills**

► **Profile of Your Related Experience**

► **Profile of Your Related Education**

► **Citation of Your Related Memberships**

YOUR CONTACT INFORMATION

Function:

- To make your identity immediately and explicitly clear
- To make it easy for the employer to contact you

Key Items for Inclusion:

- Your name
- Your street address, city, state and zip code
- Your home phone number, including the area code

Optional Item for Inclusion:

- Your work or message phone number. This is especially important if you do not have an answering machine on your home phone.

Additional Points:

- Consider using a slightly larger typeface for your name, and bold print for visual emphasis.
- Repeat your name at the top of the second page of a two-page resume.

STATEMENT OF YOUR CAREER OBJECTIVE

Function:

- To ensure that your resume is a well-focused, tightly integrated sales tool, rather than a miscellaneous summary of distracting autobiographical data
- To provide the criterion for inclusion and exclusion, emphasis and de-emphasis of everything else that follows
- To be the "drive shaft" in drafting and editing the body of your resume

Key Items for Inclusion:

- Cite functional area of expertise and interest, as in department sponsoring the contributing role.

    For example: CORPORATE FINANCE

- Give generic focus, so it will include related jobs.

  For example: HUMAN RESOURCE DEVELOPMENT

- Consider using a specific job title when you are a strongly qualified candidate for an available position.

  For example: SENIOR TRAINING SPECIALIST

- Be concise, eliminating personal agendas like ''a challenging, meaningful position . . . leading to advancement to management'' and rambling hype such as ''with compensation commensurate with contribution.''

Optional Items for Inclusion:

- Cite your functional area of expertise and interest, and related contributing roles you could play.

  For example:
  ### BUSINESS INFORMATION SYSTEMS
  • Systems Analysis • Office Automation • Programming • Computer Education

- Cite the level of responsibility you are seeking, if it is key to the assessment of your candidacy.

  For example: ''ENTRY LEVEL,'' ''SUPERVISORY'' or ''SENIOR STAFF.''

- Cite the industry you have targeted, if you have narrowed your objective to this degree.

  For example: ''HEALTH CARE,'' ''COMPUTER INDUSTRY'' or ''CPA FIRM.''

- Include one or more mission statements, showing your understanding of the core functions and purposes of the work you are seeking, crucial factors to success of your awareness of key priorities.

  For example:
  ### OCCUPATIONAL NURSE
  Consultation, Education and Treatment for Wellness in the Workplace

CAREER OBJECTIVE EXAMPLES

EXAMPLES OF CAREER OBJECTIVE

OBJECTIVE

AUDITING POSITION/CPA FIRM

OBJECTIVE

SALES REPRESENTATIVE/NUTRITIONAL PRODUCTS

OBJECTIVE

PRODUCT SUPPORT

• End User Documentation   • Customer Training

OBJECTIVE

ASSISTANT MANAGER TRAINEE

• Management Support   • Efficient Operations   • Strong Customer Service

---

OBJECTIVE

ENTRY LEVEL POSITION/ADVERTISING

Product Promotion Strategies and Campaigns
• Positioning for Visibility   • Building Profitability

OBJECTIVE

MANAGEMENT POSITION/UNIVERSITY ADMISSIONS AND RECORDS

• Systems and Procedures for Timely Processing of Applications
• Collaborative Relationships with Faculty
• Service-Oriented Dealings with Prospective and Current Students and Alumni

SUMMARY OF YOUR QUALIFICATIONS

Function:

- To create a bridge between your objective and the rest of your resume

- To be a power-packed summary of formal and informal qualifications for your objective

- To capture attention and create receptivity to the detailed information that follows

- To frame yourself in terms of how you wish to be seen, beyond the obvious facts of your experience

Key Items for Inclusion:

- Cite number of years of experience

- Cite type of experience, such as "direct," "related," "diversified," "increasingly more responsible," "business," "contributed services," "avocational," "intern," etc.

- Cite key skills and tasks that constitute themes in your qualifying experience and that support your objective

- Cite specialized studies, if applicable, referencing details later in the EDUCATION category

Optional Item for Inclusion:

- Cite relevant attitudes and personality traits that contribute to your superior performance. *For example:*

  —For a Production Inspector:
  Commitment to carefully checking details to support product quality

  —For a Plant Security Officer:
  Strong safety-consciousness, vigilance in maintaining readiness for emergencies, and promptness in responding to calls

  —For a Training Specialist:
  A leader in managing change and providing personal support in adapting to related stresses and challenges

Additional Point:

- It is often easier to write your SUMMARY *after* you complete the other sections of your draft. At that point you can extrapolate key selling points about yourself as a "lead" into the body of your resume.

EXAMPLES OF SUMMARY OF QUALIFICATIONS

OBJECTIVE

TAX INTERNSHIP

QUALIFIED BY

Specialized studies, a student leadership position using organizing, communication, and promotional skills, and work experience in meeting deadlines, doing bookkeeping, and providing client services.

OBJECTIVE

MARKETING PROFESSIONAL

QUALIFIED BY

Three years of direct, diversified and increasingly responsible experience in developing marketing strategy, and conducting and managing campaigns for corporate communications and product promotion.

OBJECTIVE

TELECOMMUNICATIONS ANALYST

QUALIFIED BY

Specialized professional studies, and nine years of corporate experience in assessing needs, designing cost-effective methods and procedures, trouble-shooting and solving workplace problems, and training employees in the use of technical products.

OBJECTIVE

PROGRAM MANAGER, OPERATIONS

QUALIFIED BY

Twenty-four years of varied decision-making experience with proficiency in managing multiple demands and pressured conditions. A lengthy track record of accountability in producing targeted results, backed by extensive engineering and business studies.

LISTING OF YOUR KEY SKILLS

Function:

- To showcase your strongest relevant abilities—elements clearly applicable or transferable to your career objective

- To establish yourself as a person who can add value—proficient, capable and effective in specific, defined ways

- To serve as a guide in filtering your experience for the most relevant supporting accomplishments to present

- To validate accomplishments from other spheres as relevant because of the transferable skills you displayed

Key Items for Inclusion:

- Cite the functional skills you do best and enjoy most—natural knacks that lend themselves to effective performance in the work you seek to do; and/or

- Cite your technical skills and special knowledge, which establishes your formal expertise in your field

Additional Points:

- Analyze your objective for key skills underlying successful performance; then thoroughly review your background for matching skills

- Sort out your primary from your secondary skills, relevant from irrelevant skills, and untangle overlapping categories

- Narrow your list to a manageable number, selecting between two and ten key skills or areas of effectiveness

- Refine the titles of your skills as needed

- Present your skills in columns or clustered phrases, set off by bullets for emphasis

---

NOTE: A listing of your key skills is highly recommended. It is not always necessary to include this as a discreet section. A strong QUALIFIED BY statement may be sufficient to showcase your skills. Whether the KEY SKILLS section warrants development is a judgment call.

Factors affecting your decision include your particular skill base, as it relates to your objective, and space constraints in the presentation of other information.

EXAMPLES OF KEY SKILLS

KEY SKILLS

- Assessing • Organizing • Innovating • Implementing • Streamlining

---

KEY SKILLS

- Consulting   • Decision Making   • Coordinating
- Troubleshooting   • Expediting

AREAS OF EFFECTIVENESS

- Event Coordination   • Multi-Media Presentations   • Customer Relations
- Promotions   • Copywriting and Editing   • Direct Sales

AREAS OF EFFECTIVENESS

- Feasibility Studies, Cost Estimates, and Proposals
- Client Presentations and Consultation
- Project and Program Management

AREAS OF EFFECTIVENESS

- Direct Nursing Care
- Health Education Counseling, Information and Referral
- Employee Evaluation/Job Assignment and Modification
- Records Management and Payment Processing

AREAS OF EFFECTIVENESS

- Cultural Services   • Public Relations
- Community Development   • Fund Raising

AREAS OF EFFECTIVENESS

- Systems and Procedures Development   • Data Processing Support
- Work Simplification   • Document Control

PROFILE OF YOUR RELATED EXPERIENCE

Function:

- To establish core reference points of your qualifying experience in objective, factual terms

- To provide employers with a clear framework for understanding you professionally and comparing you with other applicants

- To provide a basis for third part comment on the skills, responsibilities and achievements recommending you for hiring

The Strategic Handling of Your Experience

- *To optimize your experience* involves a series of creative judgment calls on how to sequence, highlight and de-emphasize various facts of your background.

- *Uncompromising honesty* is the bottom line for all representations you make about yourself. And, as any marketing professional can tell you, within the bounds of honesty, you have tremendous freedom to make the most of what you have to offer.

- A precondition to having others see the applicability of what you have done to what you want to do is *your ability to see yourself in that light*. As you approach the strategic handling of your experience, this guide provides you support on several major points:

   A. ISSUES REGARDING INCLUSION, EMPHASIS AND PERSPECTIVE

   B. TREATMENT OF YOUR CORE REFERENCE INFORMATION

   C. TREATMENT OF YOUR DESCRIPTION

   D. TREATMENT OF YOUR EXPERIENCE IN EACH RESUME FORMAT

A. ISSUES REGARDING INCLUSION, EMPHASIS AND PERSPECTIVE

Type of Experience You May Cite:

Experience from every realm of your life may be cited, clustered in groups under subtitled headings referring to the nature of the experience:

- Showcase your strongest categories of experience by sequencing them first, regardless of how recent or informal they were. *For example:*

Career-Related Employment		Internships		Consulting Contract
	or		or	
Other Business Background		Employment		Contributed Services

- Consider using header statements to strengthen weak or unrelated experience. *For example:*

    Part-Time and Temporary Jobs Financing Higher Education

Kinds of Jobs To Cite:

You only need to include professional jobs. Your resume is not a company application form, requiring you to list all employment you have held. It is a targeted sales tool, presenting a full accounting of all *relevant* positions.

For example, if you have had a well-established career, been laid off in a downsizing, and needed to do temporary interim work outside of your field at a lower level of responsibility and pay, you are not required to include this information on your resume. Measures taken to stabilize yourself financially, while searching for an appropriate position, are personal, adaptive responses to necessity. They should not dilute your candidacy and bargaining strength for a new career position.

On the other hand, if support positions have been your sole experience, or the bulk of it, over a substantial period, cite them on your resume. Delineate your employment history in terms of the most challenging responsibilities you have handled, and use these accomplishments as a bridge to career advancement.

When to Start Your Record of Experience:

Start your record of experience whenever you want. Leave the burden of initiative on the employer to probe back further if he or she wishes. However, once you begin your professional track record, you may not delete a full-time regular position, simply because it did not work out, without becoming subject to a charge of fraudulent misrepresentation and risking later dismissal.

B. TREATMENT OF YOUR CORE REFERENCE INFORMATION

Core reference information includes the skeletal facts of your employment history—positions you have held, employers you have worked for, where they are located and when you worked there.

Formula: TITLE, Organization, Location by City and State (Dates by Years Only)

TITLE:

- Use exact titles if they clearly recommend your hiring.

- Use equivalent titles if your exact title might be biasing.

- Use a function if your title or series of titles would undermine your candidacy.

- Your title is frequently the most relevant and helpful information to emphasize, highlighting your level of responsibility and/or expertise. You will usually want to capitalize it. In contrast, you will usually want to treat the name of the organization you have left or are seeking to leave without visual emphasis.

Organization, Location by City and State:

- Cite these explicitly—they represent keystones of the resume's credibility to an employer.

- A subset phrase directly underneath the core reference information may be used to clarify the nature and size of operation of the employer. Typically a one-liner and no longer than three lines, it is chiefly relevant for established managers in portraying the context of personal achievement.

Dates by Years Only:

- Give an accurate, though approximate, chronology. Leave the burden of the initiative on the employer to probe for more exact dates.

- De-emphasize any gaps in months of service, keeping the focus on your skills, knowledge and accomplishments related to your objective.

- Put dates at the end of the TITLE, Organization, Location line, or after description, to de-emphasize significance. Consider putting dates in parentheses to further visually de-emphasize them.

TREATMENT OF YOUR CORE REFERENCE INFORMATION (continued)

Format Options for Core Reference Information:

When you have had one major departmental affiliation per major employer:

TITLE, Organization, Location by City and State   (Dates by Years Only)

TITLE, Organization, Location by City and State   (Dates by Years Only)

TITLE, Organization, Location by City and State   (Dates by Years Only)

TITLE, Organization, Location by City and State   (Dates by Years Only)

When you want to trace your progression within one or more organizations:

- Organization, Location by City and State

  TITLE   (Dates by Years Only)
  TITLE   (Dates by Years Only)

- Organization, Location by City and State

  TITLE   (Dates by Years Only)
  TITLE   (Dates by Years Only)

- Organization, Location by City and State

  TITLE   (Dates by Years Only)

Additional Points:

- Cite your present or most recent job first, working backward. Exception: Delineating subclusters of experience where entries fall in chronological order under the referenced headings.

- Single space entries to minimize prominence of the nature or number of jobs you have had; otherwise, when space permits, double-space entries.

EXAMPLES OF CORE REFERENCE INFORMATION

EXPERIENCE

DEPARTMENT MANAGER TRAINEE, Filene's, Braintree, MA	(1992–Present)
BUYER, Jordan Marsh, Hanover, MA	(1990–1991)
ASSISTANT MANAGER, Connally's Children's Wear, Quincy, MA	(1988–1989)
ASSISTANT BUYER, Bradlee's, Hingham, MA	(1986–1987)

EXPERIENCE

ACCOUNTING MANAGER, Audio Futures, Atlanta, GA (1986–Present)
Electronic sound equipment manufacturer. Sales $6 million; 65 employees.

CONTROLLER, Optima, Inc., Savannah, GA (1982–1985)
Fine art retailer/wholesaler. Sales $8 million; 38 employees.

ACCOUNTANT, Industrial Glass, Miami, FL (1979–1982)
National glass manufacturer/wholesaler. 200 employees in corporate office.

EXPERIENCE

Career Related Positions:

CLIENT SERVICE ASSOCIATE, Phillips-Hill, Inc., Denver, CO	(1986–1988)
SALES MANAGER, United Parcel Service, Boulder, CO	(1981–1985)
ASSISTANT SALES MANAGER, Leemy (W.A.) Ltd., Logos, Nigeria	(1978–1980)

Employment Financing Graduate Studies:

DIRECTOR OF SECURITY, Captain's Cove, Inc., Provo, UT	(1991–Present)

EXPERIENCE

Hewlett Packard, Palo Alto, CA

SUPERVISOR, GENERAL STORES & PURCHASING	(1983–Present)
SUPERVISOR, MATERIAL CONTROL	(1976–1982)
RELATED SUPPORT POSITIONS	(1968–1975)

C. TREATMENT OF YOUR DESCRIPTION

The description information identifies your relevant record of direct or elated experience. Ground your selling points in concrete accomplishments. "For instances" that demonstrate effective performance should predict your contribution and success with a new employer.

Formula: Did what, with, or for whom, on what scale, with what results.

- *Did:* identifies the skill, consistently using the past tense that can assume present usage

- *What:* describes the task

- *With Whom:* notes colleagues or clients/customers addressed

- *For Whom:* includes contextual reference such as department, type of business, industry

- *On What Scale:* describes, in objective terms, where possible quantifying achievement—size, speed, cost, percentage, number of people, time frame etc.

- *With What Results:* defines the purpose, explicit benefits, established impact—turn-around accomplished, new business developed, liability limited, efficiency improved, volume of business expanded, etc.

Additional Points:

- Start your accomplishment statements using power-packed action verbs. Lead with the strongest words you can, to emphasize your skilled contribution.

- Avoid using the personal pronoun "I" or the possessive pronoun "my." This will keep the tone objective, crisp and professional.

- Avoid using subjective self-evaluation through adjectives like "creative," "intelligent" and "enterprising." Use strongly worded accomplishment statements so that the employer can deduce such things about you.

- Cite contextual reference of settings that are different than what you are now targeting, in generic terms that will enhance transferability. For example, describe a church as a service organization.

- Discuss your experience in terms meaningful to your target audience. For example, a retiring military officer might focus on logistics and personnel management, rather than the specifics of weapons systems. Avoid specialized jargon.

EXAMPLES OF ACCOMPLISHMENT-ORIENTED DESCRIPTION

Coordinated six fund-raisers benefitting the American Heart Association, including bike-a-thons, candy sales, and door-to-door drives. Recruited and supervised volunteers of up to 100 people, and raised over $5,000.

Earned all personal living expenses during four-year course of undergraduate study by maintenance of full-time service employment.

Fielded up to 20 customer service phone calls per day, troubleshooting problems, cutting red tape, and making special arrangements as needed to maintain good will relationships and stimulate repeat business for a retail travel agency.

Determined process bottlenecks in three production units of a heavy industrial and agricultural chemical manufacturer. Instituted process modifications that increased production by 20 percent and reduced labor and raw material costs by 30 percent.

Served as the primary provider in Quality Assurance of SPC on torque of critical fasteners, bringing enhanced ability to pinpoint faulty parts, failing tools, and ineffective areas of production processes.

Conducted a production inventory and calculated costs as a consultant to a specialty retail store; findings led to a shift in purchasing strategy.

Redesigned structure, and established key functional areas and committees for a tennis club, which resulted in a 33 percent increase in membership.

Planned the catering, set design, and marketing for 10 real estate broker open houses to promote client properties, with an attendance of 200+ each.

D. TREATMENT OF YOUR EXPERIENCE IN EACH RESUME FORMAT

"Experience" in the Chronological Resume

You can enliven the traditional, historical format. Replace the mundane, abstract and/or overly detailed description often found in chronological resumes with selective, persuasive examples of relevant accomplishments.

Formula: Reference core information for a particular job. Follow this with a brief illustrative narrative, emphasizing personal accomplishment. Repeat the sequence for each job experience.

> TITLE, organization, location by city and state (Dates by years only)
> Description—Did what with, or for whom, on what scale, with what results.
>
> TITLE, organization, location by city and state (Dates by years only)
> Description—Did what with, or for whom, on what scale, with what results.
>
> TITLE, organization, location by city and state (Dates by years only)
> Description—Did what with, or for whom, on what scale, with what results.

Additional Points:

- You may want to make a brief statement about the nature and scope of your personal responsibilities as a context for subsequent bulleted accomplishments, highlighting your personal excellence and contribution in the job.

- Each experience you cite can take the form of a responsibility summary with modifying accomplishments, or of one or more freestanding accomplishments. Treatment can vary on the same resume from reference to reference.

"Experience" in the Functional Resume

You can present the core structure of your experience in immediate satisfaction of an employer's need for the "big picture" of your background, while elaborating on your related track record. The format should minimize any marketability issues and accent your contribution and success.

Formula: **List core reference information job-by-job, under the heading EXPERIENCE. Do not include other elaborating information in this section.**

TITLE, organization, location by city and state (Dates—years only)

TITLE, organization, location by city and state (Dates—years only)

TITLE, organization, location by city and state (Dates—years only)

Descriptions are contained under a separate category with the heading "RELATED ACCOMPLISHMENTS."

- "Did what, with, or for whom, on what scale, with what results" provides the structure for writing your accomplishments.

- Your Related Accomplishments may come from any arena of your life experience, as long as you have a reference point somewhere on your resume.

- Be selective in what you cite, showcasing only your most senior and relevant experience. This means that many elements of a particular job may not be cited, whole jobs may not merit description, and some part-time, brief, unpaid, avocational and other such experience may be given status.

- As explicitly as possible, link your selected "for instances" to your Key Skills.

- Ensure that all of your Key Skills appear in your Related Accomplishments.

- Do not be concerned about having a separate Related Accomplishment for every Key Skill cited. In some cases, a Related Accomplishment will illustrate two or more of your Key Skills; this may occur one or more times.

- When clearcut parallels can be established, match the sequencing of your Related Accomplishments to the sequencing of your Key Skills.

PROFILE OF YOUR RELATED EDUCATION

Function:

To establish credit and noncredit credentials, completed or in progress, that testify to your relevant knowledge base.

Key Items for Inclusion:

- Degrees completed or in progress—Variations on status of degree:

    Level of degree, FOCUS OF DEGREE, Year of completion

    Level of degree, FOCUS OF DEGREE—In Progress. Completion: x Semester, 199–

    Level of degree, FOCUS OF DEGREE—In Progress. x units or x percent completed

    Level of degree, FOCUS OF DEGREE—Studies in Progress

- Second Line of Information:

    Degree-granting institution, location by city and state

Additional Points:

- Cite your most recent degree in progress or completed, then work backward in time.

- Delete any reference to an associate degree when a bachelor degree is completed.

- Delete any reference to high school diploma when an associate degree is completed.

- Visually emphasize the focus of the degree, rather than the degree-granting institution. Exception: when the degree-granting institution is so prestigious that accenting it is a major leveraging factor.

- Delete the focus of your undergraduate degree if it varies from your present objective, or if it may bias your target audience. *For example:* when targeting business jobs, do not focus on Elementary Education, Theology, etc.

Optional Items for Inclusion:

- Additional categories, or further delineation of degrees, such as:

    Honors and Awards; Leadership Positions; Professional Development Seminars; Employer-Sponsored Training; Certificates; Licensing Status; Related Course Work.

EXAMPLES OF EDUCATION

EDUCATION

GRADUATE, Albany High School, Albany, CA

Employer-Sponsored Training: Dale Carnegie Course

EDUCATION

Three years of coursework leading to a Bachelor of Arts degree
Rutgers University, New Brunswick, NJ

Master Electrician, State of New Jersey

Employer-Sponsored Training:

MANAGEMENT/SUPERVISION
- Certificate in Management
- Manufacturing Supervision
- Meeting Leadership
- Communication Skills:
  Assertiveness; Business Writing

TECHNICAL
- Management Overview of Robotics
- Cincinnati Milacron Robotics Operations
- SQ-0 Microprocessor Welder Control
- Programmable Controller Operations:
  Allen-Bradley; Gould Modicon; SQ-0 881

EDUCATION

BA, 1990. Loyola University, Chicago, IL

Leadership Positions:
Award-Winning Public Speaker; Captain of Tennis Team;
Community Council Representative

EDUCATION

MBA, FINANCE, 1989. Suffolk University, Boston, MA

Earned while working full-time. GPA: 3.84
Coursework Emphases: Economic Forecasting and Capital Budgeting

BA, PSYCHOLOGY, 1979. Boston College, Chestnut Hill, MA

CITATION OF YOUR RELATED MEMBERSHIPS

Function:

- To carry your professional identity full circle:

  —from establishing your focus in the OBJECTIVE

  —to distilling your major selling points in the QUALIFIED BY section

  —to profiling your power-packed KEY SKILLS

  —to direct or related EXPERIENCE and EDUCATION descriptions

  —through relevant professional affiliations

- To create a subliminal identification of "I am one of you," in touch with the state-of-the-art developments and key issues in the field, etc.

- To support access to colleagues who can be helpful to you in your networking initiatives.

Key Items for Inclusion:

- National and local professional groups in your functional and/or industry interest areas.

- *The Encyclopedia of Professional Associations,* readily available in libraries, is a good source for national groups. You can join local chapters of national groups at moderate fees, which may be tax deductable.

- Networking is a good source of information on local professional organizations, which are often cohesive, informal and vital groups of significant value.

- List any offices held or major service roles performed for professional groups in which you have been active.

- List any honors or awards bestowed upon you for distinctive performance in your profession.

EXAMPLES AHEAD

EXAMPLES OF MEMBERSHIPS

MEMBERSHIP

International Association of Business Communications

MEMBERSHIPS

- American Marketing Association
- National Transportation Society

MEMBERSHIP

American Bankers Association
Program Chair, Continuing Education Division

MEMBERSHIP

American Society for Training and Development

Winner of Chapter Award for Innovative Leadership, 1992
Community Service Committee Member

MEMBERSHIP

Institute of Electrical and Electronics Engineers

Conference Presentation:
''Evolution of 19mm Magnetic Tape Standards for Video,
Instrumentation and Data Processing''
Tenth IEEE Symposium on Mass Storage

MEMBERSHIP

Data Processing Management Association

Elected Leadership Positions:
Board of Directors (1988–Present); Vice President (1990–1991); Secretary (1991–1992)

STEP 6: REFINE THE QUALITY

At this point, your task is to refine what you have written. Closely scrutinize your draft for every enhancement. Bring a gently critical perspective to examine it from every angle. Use a red pen or pencil to flag items you want to improve, change the emphasis, or delete.

Picture yourself as the hiring manager for a job you want. Does the substance of the resume catch your attention? Are you impressed by what you read? Does it match a profile of the kind of person you could use on your staff? Does it create interest in getting together for an exploratory meeting? Would you schedule an interview on the basis of this resume?

Now, picture yourself as an editor. Are you satisfied that there are no errors on the resume? Does it hang together tightly? Does it seem organized in the most effective way? Is it easy and inviting to read? Would you sign off on this resume as a top-notch example of effective writing?

Editing Checklist

Selectivity:

☐ Do the items on your resume support your objective?

☐ Have you de-emphasized experiences that are not clearly qualifying?

☐ Have you eliminated extraneous information like marital status and age?

☐ Does the language you use enhance your marketability?

Sequencing:

☐ Are your strongest categories presented first?

☐ Are the strongest items within your categories presented first?

☐ Do your headings and subheadings bring out your key selling points?

Tone:

☐ Is your language upbeat?

☐ Do you begin your sentences with strong action verbs?

☐ Have you avoided using personal pronouns?

Specificity:

☐ Do you focus on facts, offering concrete ''for instances'' of your strengths?

☐ Do you use written numeric figures to quantify your achievements?

☐ Do you use other objective measures when figures are not applicable?

Clarity:

☐ Are your thoughts well-organized, in clear sentences and paragraphs?

☐ Have you avoided jargon?

☐ Have you avoided abbreviations?

Simplicity:

☐ Do you use short words, sentences and paragraphs?

☐ Have you cut out redundancies?

☐ Can you condense, consolidate or delete anything for greater impact?

Consistency:

☐ Is your capitalization consistent?

☐ Are your verb tenses consistent?

☐ Do items of a similar nature have parallel structures?

Accuracy:

☐ Have you eliminated typographical errors?

☐ Is your spelling correct?

☐ Is your punctuation correct?

☐ Is your grammar correct?

STEP 7: PACKAGE WITH CARE

A resume that looks sharp gets attention and stimulates interest in its substance. When the content is in top-notch shape, your final task is to package it. Match the verbal standard you have set for yourself with an equally high visual standard. Let graphics help sell you.

Picture yourself in a first class advertising agency, charged with packaging your resume in a tasteful, effective form. No frills, no gimmicks, just a quietly distinctive statement reflecting classic design principles. What criteria would you bring to set-up the text? What would you watch out for and be careful not to do? How would you develop camera-ready master copy?

Now picture yourself as the production manager of the creative department. What printing process would you use? What paper would you select? What quality control measures would you take to ensure that every copy of the resume is crisp and clear?

Packaging Checklist

Overall Impact:

☐ Does your resume make a positive impression at first glance?

☐ Do the graphics enhance the communication of the information?

☐ Is it easy to find your crucial selling points?

Page Layout:

☐ Have you selected the standard 8½″ × 11″ size for your page?

☐ Have you determined the relative merits of major formats for your needs—of left margin headings, centered headings or left margin headings with text underneath?

☐ Have you been consistent in your placement of headings and subheadings?

☐ Have you avoided justifying the right margin so that words are evenly spaced?

☐ Have you eliminated single words at the end of paragraphs and page starts?

☐ Have you used vertical spacing consistently, establishing well-defined groupings of information?

Highlighting:

- [ ] Have you made selective use of various techniques of emphasis, such as bolding, capitalization, bullets, underlining, punctuation, headings and subheadings?

- [ ] Have you bolded and capitalized your name and major category headings?

- [ ] Have you used upper- and lowercase lettering in text entries, for readability?

- [ ] Have you made liberal use of bullets as the primary method of accenting brief, important entries like key skills and accomplishments?

- [ ] Have you used colons, dashes and slashes to your advantage?

- [ ] Have you used headings to guide the reader through the major components of your qualifications, sequenced in order of importance?

- [ ] Have you used subheadings to spotlight groupings of qualifications of special importance, distinct from those of relative unimportance?

Typography:

- [ ] Have you focused on a time-tested classic typeface—a sans serif like Helvetica or a serif like Times Roman?

- [ ] Have you limited yourself to a maximum of two typefaces, to avoid clutter and competition for attention with the message of your text?

- [ ] Have you sized your typeface for text between 9 and 12 points?

- [ ] Have you used a carbon ribbon if your means of text set-up is a typewriter?

- [ ] Have you used a laser or ink jet printer if you've word processed your resume?

- [ ] Have you written explicit, detailed design specifications if you're using typesetting?

- [ ] Have you proofread your master copy with rigorous care to ensure it is precisely as you wish, with no typos, misspellings, or other problems?

Paper:

- [ ] Have you selected a high quality bond paper, with a high cotton fiber content?

- [ ] Have you chosen white, ivory, beige or light grey for your paper color?

Printing:

- [ ] Have you selected a printing process for quality reproduction—using either an offset duplicator or an offset press?

STEP 8: RUN A QUALITY CHECK

Above and beyond your own careful editorial and packaging review, you may want to introduce one final quality assurance measure. It is often useful to evaluate your resume through the eyes of one or more of your valued colleagues.

Consider contacts whose professional judgment you regard highly. Request a candid assessment of your resume. Explain that you have given considerable time and thought to developing a strong statement about yourself to support your new career horizons, and are substantially satisfied with its overall design.

Explain that you want to be sure that you have not overlooked anything that could affect its positive impact in your job search. You would appreciate any input that could enhance what you have produced.

Feedback from someone who is experienced in the career area you are pursuing is particularly valuable. You can count on solid understanding of the nature of the work, knowledge of important skills and insight on the kind of experiences that may be most useful to emphasize.

A Caution

In a room of ten people, you will be apt to find ten different opinions about what makes a good resume. There is a wide variety of perspectives on this subject. Many people subscribe to very conventional ways of presenting written qualifications. It may not be in your best interest to incorporate every suggestion.

The key point is to value your own judgment in filtering the ideas you receive. Make only those alterations that truly improve how you present yourself.

Field testing your resume is good solid marketing practice. It has the potential to provide excellent advice for fine-tuning your resume.

Build in what you think is best. Then use your resume with confidence and enjoyment.

5

Using Your Resume for Optimal Results

STRATEGIC JOB SEEKING

With your strategic resume in hand, your task broadens. The same type of thinking that is crucial in your resume production is equally vital in your other job search activities. Using your resume for optimal results involves a constant assessment of factors that may help and hinder you and a series of practical judgment calls on the most appropriate action.

Evaluating your personal preparedness for job seeking is a good first step. Your confidence will be reinforced as you recognize what you already have going for you. And, on tasks that require some attention, you will be off to a good start in deciding where to focus.

A Personal Preparedness Checklist

On a scale of 1 through 5 (1=Low; 5=High), code each of the statements below with the number that best reflects your job search readiness.

_____ I have a positive attitude about marketing myself.

_____ I have a strong support system for maintaining momentum.

_____ I have a clear and realistic job objective.

_____ I have an effective strategic resume.

_____ I have a clear idea of how to write effective cover letters.

_____ I have planning and record-keeping systems set up to maximize my efficiency.

_____ I have a list of people I plan to consult for information and advice.

_____ I have a list of employers I am interested in approaching.

_____ I have at least basic company information on my target employers.

_____ I have a good understanding of networking benefits and techniques.

_____ I have a good knowledge of sources of job leads in my line of work.

_____ I have a solid grasp of job interviewing methods and issues.

_____ I have proficiency in communicating in job interviews.

_____ I have several strong references who can respond to inquiries.

_____ I have a solid grounding in salary negotiation techniques.

_____ I have clear criteria for evaluating the merits of specific job offers.

Strategy Day-by-Day

The most challenging part of strategic job-seeking comes up in day-to-day experience. The old maxim, "Expect the unexpected" applies. All kinds of unpredictable situations are likely to arise, which require positive perspective, quick thinking and resourcefulness.

Your job search may be complicated by conditions that have nothing to do with you personally. For example, an employer may:

- Reevaluate filling an advertised position because of a budget crunch
- Put a prospective project, that you were slated to do, on hold indefinitely
- Lose a key contract that would have provided funding for additional staffing
- Be acquired by another company or become the focus of a hostile takeover bid
- Undertake restructuring that eliminates a key contact you have cultivated

In addition to internal organizational issues, you may encounter subjective barriers to opportunity. For example, key decision-makers may have attitudes and hiring practices that adversely affect your candidacy. These include:

- A premium placed on prior direct experience
- A priority placed on a different skills set
- A preference for a different style
- A policy to hire from within (or from outside)
- A tradition of hiring someone very different from you in age, gender or ethnicity

These factors and many more are typical challenges during a job search. At first glance, there may seem to be little reason for optimism. It can be perilously easy to fall into negative thinking, frustration or resignation.

Obstacles as a Point of Departure

In strategic job seeking, predictable and unpredictable problems are a given. All-or-nothing, now-or-never thinking is rejected. Instead, obstacles inspire creative problem solving and proposal making, and probing for other possibilities that may exist or be developed.

The ingenuity called upon in writing a strategic resume is called for again and again in the successful conduct of a personal marketing campaign. It is a consistent way of thinking about careers that is pragmatic about the problems and dedicated to solutions.

AN EMPHASIS ON NETWORKING

As you position yourself for a new career opportunity, you may decide to draw upon a wide repertoire of job search methods. You can especially benefit from varied approaches if you are clearly well-qualified for the work you seek, with a direct track record of applicable job experience.

Obvious channels of information about jobs include advertisements, agencies or search firms, and personnel offices. They are not hard to find and focus on filling budgeted openings. Perhaps you know people who have found jobs this way. Maybe you have landed a job yourself using these resources.

If a traditional method of job search works for you, great! If you become aware of a special position that seems made to order, go for it! Opportunity may come from many different sources, all valid are worthwhile to explore, all potentially productive.

HOWEVER, experts say that about 80 percent of jobs are found through the hidden job market, the informal channels of communication between employers and job seekers. What conclusions might you draw about preferred job search strategy?

The Case for Networking

If you place a premium on matching yourself with compatible roles and settings . . .

If you value keeping the initiative as you conduct your search for work . . .

If you want to access more job opportunity than standard sources publicize . . .

If you would like to position yourself favorably with people with power to hire . . .
NETWORKING WILL BE FOR YOU!

Networking, in plain and simple terms, means reaching out to other people for advice, information, feedback and referrals. It is an informal exploration of possible opportunities. It builds bridges to find out about needs you can meet, and is a mechanism for talking with people you would probably never know about or get through if you were to use more formal job search methods.

Networking gives you tremendous freedom to target where you would really like to work, meet outside of competitive selection processes, find out about real and compelling hiring needs. You gain the interest of key people who can hire you, open doors for you, or leverage yourself to be hired by friends and colleagues.

Through traditional job search means, you find out about a limited slice of opportunity. This is heavily tended by gatekeepers whose primary function is to screen out anyone but the most obviously, formidably, well-qualified candidates.

Through networking, you find out about posted openings and get a helping hand in competing for them. AND you find out about employment options that are not yet published, budget requisitions in the pipeline for authorization, operating needs in departments that will shortly be the source of staffing requests, and problems you could address as a temporary consultant. To use your resume for optimal results, consider the benefits of networking as you plan your own job search strategy.

THEORIES ON TIMING

The best time to present your resume to a prospective employer or referral source is a hotly debated topic in career counseling circles. Experienced practitioners hold varying views. The divergent thinking in this area underscores a very important point: there is no categorical right or wrong on this and many other job search questions.

What works for you is what is important. Defining that may take some personal reflection and experimentation. It may also mean making case-by-case judgment calls, assessing what in a particular instance makes the most sense to you.

The Send-It-Ahead Theory—This theory holds that your resume plays a key role in paving the way for a personal interview. It emphasizes the benefit of giving a concise, well-crafted statement about yourself, in a form that honors an employer's time. He or she can review it, as convenient, and be motivated to want to talk with you. Sent with a carefully written cover letter, hopefully with a referral to reinforce receptivity, it sets a positive tone and positions you to get through on a follow-up phone call about an exploratory meeting.

The Leave-It-Behind Theory—This theory holds that it is best to approach employers through the spoken word. It emphasizes telephone calls that are carefully thought through, while informal in style. It makes direct personal contact critical, and assumes a fairly assertive person to get through to people you do not already know. The resume serves as a positive reminder of experiences you share in conversation, and a reference point to share with others involved in a staffing process.

The Send-It-Afterward Theory—This theory is closely allied with the leave-it-behind theory, but takes the process much further. It holds that your resume should precisely reflect the needs discovered in conversation with a prospective employer; you tailor your resume in fine detail to that specific job possibility. Situational relevance is the primary writing principle for custom-designed communications with each and every employer you approach seriously.

The Don't-Send-It-Unless-Asked Theory—This theory has a couple of variations. Send a tailored letter of approach without a resume, emphasizing relevant accomplishments. Keep your resume available in case the employer wants it for supplemental information. OR keep all communication on an oral basis to maximize interaction and feedback. In this case you can send your resume ahead, leave it behind, or follow up with a resume only to accommodate a specific request.

Trust your instincts, your intuition, your own best judgment in deciding what to do. For best results, stay observant and flexible.

VALUE-ADDING LETTERS

Using your resume for optimal results will sometimes involve letter writing. Like your resume, letters can be written on a very routine level or with high positive impact. At a minimum, a letter serves as a conveyance of your resume. At its best, a letter adds value, communicates information over and above your resume, which assists in positioning you for opportunity.

Personalized Communications

In sharp contrast to boilerplate generalities, a value-adding letter is a personalized communication. It emerges out of very careful consideration of what you want to say to a particular person, who is a potential resource in your job search.

First and foremost of course, a value-adding letter *always* begins with the name of the intended recipient. It is always addressed to a specific person you have identified as beneficial to contact. It recognizes that hiring is a very personal process enhanced by personal contact at every step of the way.

Tailored Communications

A value-adding letter recognizes that individual recipients have individualized concerns. It shows an understanding of a particular context, a special set of conditions, a major emphasis of work. It makes explicit links between what you have done and what you would like to do, describing especially relevant experiences in more detail than the resume alone can usually accommodate.

It is a valuable opportunity to bring out your enthusiasm for the work you seek, to show an understanding of an employer's priorities and concerns, and to spotlight certain personal qualities and background elements that make you notably well-qualified to contribute.

Persuasive Communications

Your basic purpose in writing is to stimulate interest and involvement. You want to tap someone to think along with you on opening up possibilities for new employment. You want to motivate someone to consider hiring you or opening doors with others with hiring needs. You want to convince someone to advise you, introduce you, recommend you, sponsor you . . .

So, consider carefully what you want to say and how you want to say it. Think hard about what information you can provide, what points you can emphasize, what language you can select to create allies and advocates for your initiatives.

A Broad Formula for Effectiveness

Whether you are making a networking contact, a direct approach to a hiring manager in a company you'd like to join, or a contact with an internal or external recruiter for a specific job, there is a basic composition process that will serve you well.

Take time to define your message, beginning with very open-ended thinking about possible content. Travel with the question, "What could add value to my resume for this particular purpose, with this specific person?"

This step lays the groundwork for your letter. It zeroes in on selecting the most important and relevant aspects of your experience. It focuses on substance—what matters most to bring up, what sheds light on your motivation to move in a particular direction, what brings out your strengths?

Once you have a handle on what you want to say, aim for a compact, power-packed statement. Build it step-by-step, from preliminary jottings to fine-tuning of the details.

▶ Brainstorm what you would like to say.

▶ Create an outline of your thoughts.

▶ Write a rough draft.

▶ Edit your letter for any refinements you can make.

▶ When possible, get an editorial review.

Some Specific Guidelines

- Make sure that your contact information is accurate and complete.

- Define your reader—what concerns or interests is he or she likely to have?

- Define your focus—what is your objective in writing a particular letter?

- Be brief while being thorough—write only one page maximum whenever possible.

- Be personal, but not inappropriately informal.

- Avoid hackneyed phrases.

- Find an editor for comments on substance, style, clarity and technical correctness.

- Make the appearance of your letter as strong as the content.

- Develop a filing system for ready reference.

STRUCTURING YOUR MESSAGE

IN YOUR INTRODUCTION

- Make a connection with your reader.

  Mention a prior contact or referral; reference an article written or a talk given; identify your response to an ad, etc.

- Define your purpose in writing.

  State your interest in an exploratory meeting or in following up on a preliminary contact; state your availability for an advertised position, etc.

IN THE BODY OF YOUR LETTER

- Provide a concise statement of the experience base you want to leverage.

  Number of years of experience in all aspects of . . . ; a recent degree in . . . ; extensive avocational pursuit of . . . ; services contributed in . . . , etc.

- Express your enthusiasm.

  Use phrases such as "highly committed to . . ."; "a real passion for . . ."; "lifelong interest in . . ."; "what I most enjoy . . ."; "very appealing to . . ."; "very motivating and rewarding to . . ."; "feel aligned with . . ."; etc.

- Provide details specific to recipient's needs and interests.

  Highlight selected accomplishments; key themes in your prior work, applicable to your new focus; experiences from any area of your life that qualify and motivate you . . .

- Refer to your resume.

  Use an introductory phrase such as: For your review, I am enclosing a copy of my resume . . . ; a profile of the "big picture" of my background . . . ; a detailed review . . .

IN YOUR CONCLUSION

- State your appreciation.

  Express, for example: Many thanks for . . . ; your availability to meet . . . ; your advice and perspective on . . . ; consideration of my candidacy . . . ; your thoughtfulness in . . .

- Establish the next step.

  State your interest clearly: I look forward to an opportunity to talk with you in the near future. I will call you in a few days to see if we could arrange a time to meet . . . I welcome the opportunity for a personal interview to discuss the strengths of my background and the range of contributing roles I could play . . .

A SAMPLER OF VALUE-ADDING LETTERS

Networking

Alex Coughlin
52 Orchard Ridge Road
Bridgeport, CT 06601
(203) 576-0138

Mr. Maurice Wilson, Sales Manager
Premium Soccer Lines, Ltd.
6642 Lincoln Boulevard
New York, NY 10010   July 14, 199X

Dear Mr. Wilson,

I am writing to you on the referral of Peter Strauss. In a recent
conversation, he suggested it could be valuable to meet with you for
your advice on developing a career in sales of soccer products, and to
explore the possibility of a contributing role at Premium Soccer Lines.

I appreciate that you may not have an opening currently, nor know of
one elsewhere. I would, however, find it valuable to talk with you
for whatever perspective you may be able to give me on developing
employment in this line of work.

Soccer is a real passion for me, and I am extremely interested in
focusing my career activities in this industry. I am very much at home
in soccer circles, and believe that peak performance comes from doing
what you most enjoy.

After years of playing a key role in a successful family business, I'm
ready to move on to a career situation that really capitalizes on my
own major enthusiasms--and that brings me to your door. For your
review, I'm enclosing a copy of my resume.

I look forward to an opportunity to talk with you in the near future,
and will call you early next week to see if we could arrange a time
to meet.

Sincerely,

Direct Approach to Hiring Manager

Frank Morrison
165 Hyacinth Circle
Lake Forest, IL 60045
(708) 234-0216

Mr. Vincent Rakowski
Director of Engineering
Kramer Construction, Ltd.
987 Johnson Rd.
Chicago, IL 60605   March 4, 199X

Dear Mr. Rakowski,

I read with interest your recent article in the IEEE journal on
Engineering Management Strategies in the New Workplace. My own
experience in technical support roles echoes many of the points you
made about adaptivity, the need for continual learning, and
interdisciplinary work teams.

I am writing to explore the possibility of employment on current or
prospective projects undergoing direction. My sixteen years of
experience in all aspects of piping construction equip me to take on
significant responsibilities and deliver results reliably, quickly
and with a high level of skill.

In a career of domestic and international project assignments with
multinational client companies, I have developed seasoned judgment in
installing piping in every major industrial application. I am able to
work under conditions of heavy time pressure, and am skilled in the
communications a successful project requires, both with engineering
staff and with the piping and welding crews.

I am enclosing my resume for your review. I welcome the opportunity
for a personal interview to discuss a match between your staffing
needs and my qualifications.

I will call you next week to check with you on your availability to
discuss pending projects I could support.

Sincerely,

Response to Ad

Evelyn Emerson
4263 Evergreen Rd.
Hingham, MA 02043
(617) 749-4629

Ms. Jane Parker, Executive Director
Parkhurst Community Center
72 Singer Avenue
Quincy, MA 02169   May 2, 199X

Dear Ms. Parker,

Your ad for a Director of Elder Services caught my eye. I am interested in being a candidate for the position, and enclose my resume for your review.

I have had a lifelong interest in community service programs, with extensive personal involvement in both volunteer and professional capacities. It would be a meaningful and rewarding experience to affiliate with Parkhurst Community Center and to contribute my skills to supporting elder services there.

As an elder myself, I feel sensitive to the needs and issues of elders, and committed to responsive services and programs. I'd value directing my time and effort to continue the very strong programs you currently offer, and exploring with center staff and participants any new areas that might be of interest.

Thank you for your consideration of my candidacy. I look forward to an opportunity to interview with you on the priorities you have in staffing the Elder Services Program and the contributing roles that I could play.

Sincerely,

Specialized Resources on Letters

A number of recent publications deal exclusively with job search correspondence. These include a variety of samples, including but not limited to how to use your resume for optimal results. The letters vary widely in language style and agenda. Their key value is to provide a broad frame of reference for your own composition initiatives. These include

- *The Perfect Cover Letter* by Richard H. Beatty
- *Dynamic Cover Letters* by Katharine Hansen with Randall Hansen
- *200 Letters for Job Hunters* by William S. Frank

A DYNAMIC DOCUMENT

Strategic resume writing is an on-going process. You may craft a splendid sales tool that represents you well in the job market at a certain time for a certain type of work. You may find that it is a very productive resource for achieving important short-term career goals.

Still, there is a built-in obsolescence to the information. It is a snapshot of your excellence up through *today*. By the very nature of what a resume is designed to do—help you to acquire a new job opportunity—it loses value as soon as it proves its value.

As your experience base broadens, you will need to revisit what is important to say about yourself on your resume. As your career goals evolve, you will need to take a fresh look at how to build the most convincing case for your candidacy for different or more senior work opportunities. As you progress, you will have new achievements to cite. As you develop additional qualifications, you will want to showcase them to full advantage.

A Continuing Design Process

At its best, your resume will change focus and form to reflect your emerging interests and strengths. The design that works for you at the entry point in your career may be limited in its ability to help you to advance. You may decide to treat certain experiences in a substantially different way, as time passes and you acquire more directly relevant qualifications. Or you may decide to make a career change in a dramatically new direction.

Using your resume for optimal results means revising it as often and as extensively as your situation warrants. It means looking at your resume as an evolving reflection of your career, redesigned as needed to feature the best of your ongoing growth and development.

A DYNAMIC DOCUMENT (continued)

Quick and Easy Changes Through Word Processing

Emerging technology has made it very simple to do everything from small fine-tunings of your resume to major reformulations. Word processing software on a personal computer allows you incredible flexibility to add, delete, rephrase and resequence information about yourself. Experimenting with different ways of framing the facts of your experience is amazingly easy. Developing different versions of your resume for specialized purposes is a simple and straightforward matter.

As a tool for both design and production, word processing provides an efficient way of generating relevant and up-to-date statements of your professional identity. It is a very special, very useful resource for producing state-of-the-art resumes in content and graphics.

CONCLUSION

Strategic Resume Benefits

Your reward for investing your time, effort and careful thinking in producing your strategic resume will be a thoroughly professional statement of your greatest strengths and interests. You develop enhanced personal confidence in your marketability. And you build a base for heightened success in the interview process.

Every strategic judgment call you make as you develop your resume reinforces a powerful way of thinking about your career and qualifications. Far beyond a narration of your biography, you have an opportunity to creatively frame the relevant facts of your background, to your best advantage.

Employers look for recruits who are focused, have track records that predict success, and are motivated to deliver peak performance. The process of developing your strategic resume is a foundation step in portraying how you are a valuable resource. The results demonstrate why there is merit in your candidacy, and how an employer stands to gain by hiring you.

Enjoy your strategic resume. Give yourself flexibility in using it. Treat it as a key auxiliary aid in making yourself known to employers. As you put it into use, continue making strategic judgment calls on when, how and with whom you will present it. Use it to position yourself for opportunity.

A Big Picture Perspective on Strategic Resumes

Above all, even as you value your resume as a major resource in your job search initiatives, keep aware of its place in your overall marketing campaign. Remember that the selection process is a matching process that examines what you cite in your resume, and much more.

Give the same effort to your interview preparation that you give to your resume preparation. You will want to communicate at the same level of excellence in the dynamic exchange of face-to-face meetings. Skill in written and oral communication is crucial for job search success.

P A R T

6

Strategic Resume Samples

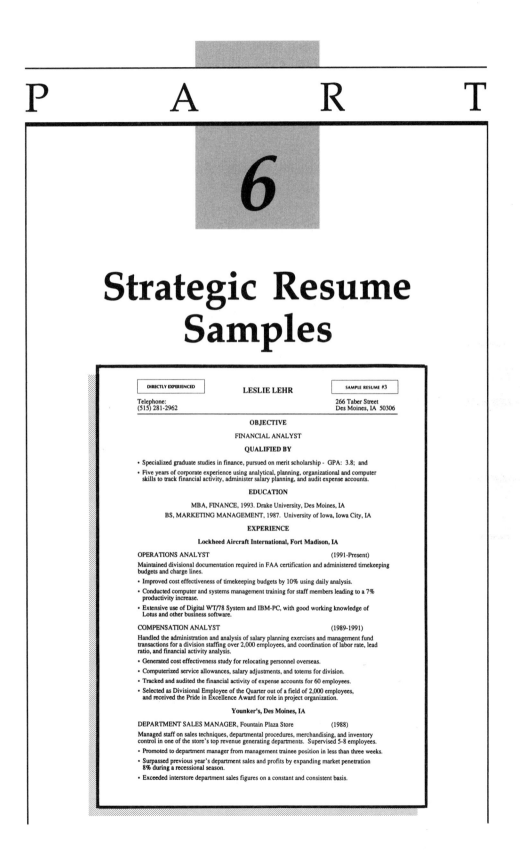

DIRECTLY EXPERIENCED	LESLIE LEHR	SAMPLE RESUME #3

Telephone:
(515) 281-2962

266 Taber Street
Des Moines, IA 50306

OBJECTIVE

FINANCIAL ANALYST

QUALIFIED BY

- Specialized graduate studies in finance, pursued on merit scholarship - GPA: 3.8; and
- Five years of corporate experience using analytical, planning, organizational and computer skills to track financial activity, administer salary planning, and audit expense accounts.

EDUCATION

MBA, FINANCE, 1993. Drake University, Des Moines, IA

BS, MARKETING MANAGEMENT, 1987. University of Iowa, Iowa City, IA

EXPERIENCE

Lockheed Aircraft International, Fort Madison, IA

OPERATIONS ANALYST   (1991-Present)

Maintained divisional documentation required in FAA certification and administered timekeeping budgets and charge lines.

- Improved cost effectiveness of timekeeping budgets by 10% using daily analysis.
- Conducted computer and systems management training for staff members leading to a 7% productivity increase.
- Extensive use of Digital WT/78 System and IBM-PC, with good working knowledge of Lotus and other business software.

COMPENSATION ANALYST   (1989-1991)

Handled the administration and analysis of salary planning exercises and management fund transactions for a division staffing over 2,000 employees, and coordination of labor rate, lead ratio, and financial activity analysis.

- Generated cost effectiveness study for relocating personnel overseas.
- Computerized service allowances, salary adjustments, and totems for division.
- Tracked and audited the financial activity of expense accounts for 60 employees.
- Selected as Divisional Employee of the Quarter out of a field of 2,000 employees, and received the Pride in Excellence Award for role in project organization.

Younker's, Des Moines, IA

DEPARTMENT SALES MANAGER, Fountain Plaza Store   (1988)

Managed staff on sales techniques, departmental procedures, merchandising, and inventory control in one of the store's top revenue generating departments. Supervised 5-8 employees.

- Promoted to department manager from management trainee position in less than three weeks.
- Surpassed previous year's department sales and profits by expanding market penetration 8% during a recessional season.
- Exceeded interstore department sales figures on a constant and consistent basis.

INTRODUCTION

Before plunging into producing your own resume, you may find it useful to review some sample resumes which illustrate the key points of your guide. Forty-four resumes are included in this section, indexed in various ways for your convenience.

Pinpointing Relevant Samples

The **Master Index** provides you a quick overview of the complete strategic resume sample base. It is coded by number, name, objective and format. You'll note that the primary principle of organization of the samples addresses the two basic situations a job-hunter potentially faces:

1. seeking a job supported by direct experience; or

2. seeking a job as a career-changer.

For a particularly dramatic illustration of the concept of strategic resumes, you may find it of special interest to examine the cluster of samples in the section entitled "Different Objectives/Different Resumes."

The **Directly Experienced Index** identifies resume samples of people dealing with career progression through pursuit of continuing areas of interest, as well as of those dealing with career renewal through a return to earlier areas of interest.

The **Career-Changing Index** identifies resume samples of launched professionals moving into new areas, as well as of support staff moving into entry level professional positions. In both cases, the point of departure for the targeted change is noted along with the new objective. It vividly underlines the scale of change it is possible to make as a career-changer through creative reframing of personal qualifications.

The **Contributing Role Index** identifies a selected sampling of resumes in several major areas of specialization in business, including production, marketing services, financial services, and varied management support advisory services. A small number of sample resumes from other sectors of the world of work is also included.

Supporting Your Objective—The Key to a Strategic Resume

Because of the almost infinite variety of specialized roles and settings, you may not find a sample directly related to your own specialty. *What is important is the way structure and strategy are used to support the objective.*

DIFFERENT OBJECTIVES/DIFFERENT RESUMES

Strategic Thinking—The Key to Tailoring Resumes

This section of sample resumes most clearly illustrates the concept of the stategic resume by presenting to you two resumes of the same person. Each of the people featured decided to pursue different career objectives concurrently, objectives consistent with their interests and strengths but responsive to different marketplace needs.

In some cases, they had no direct experience in either or any of the areas of work sought. In other cases, a job search in the area of current or recent employment was planned along with one in an area of either earlier or new interest.

Strategic Thinking—The Key to Selling

The career challenge was to relate to the concerns and to speak the language of the target audience. Hence, from different objectives, different resumes. Depending upon how different the objectives were, the resumes ranged from moderately to extremely different in the nature, sequencing and grouping of information presented.

Each and every difference was the result of a careful assessment and strategic judgement call on what would best support the objective stated at the top of the resume. That objective was all-determining on what to include or emphasize, and correspondingly, what to exclude or deemphasize. In all cases, creative positioning for favorable consideration went hand in hand with honest representation of the facts.

Strategic Thinking—A Practical Exercise

To facilitate easy comparison of the resumes of each person featured, the samples in this section have been placed side-by-side. Take a look at Molly's resume, and those of Jesse, Joan, Sonny and Rita . . .

Observe what is the same and what is different. Consider why certain components are handled differently, and how this handling strengthens each resume as a sales tool. From this process of comparison and analysis, you'll sharpen your ability to think strategically about resume writing, to apply to your own situation in writing your draft.

MASTER INDEX

DIRECTLY EXPERIENCED

CAREER-CHANGING

DIFFERENT OBJECTIVES/DIFFERENT RESUMES

35	CORBETT, MOLLY	Travel and Tourism Marketing Support	Funct.
36	CORBETT, MOLLY	Writer/Editor: Corporate Communications	Funct.
37	HANIFY, JESSE	Secondary School Teaching/Grades 7–12	Funct.
38	HANIFY, JESSE	Product Support/Customer Service	Funct.
39	BUCKLEY, JOAN	Technical Training/HR Software Packages	Chron.
40	BUCKLEY, JOAN	Employment Counselor	Funct.
41	PETRAS, SONNY	Management Position/Admissions and Records	Chron.
42	PETRAS, SONNY	Auditing Position/CPA Firm	Funct.
43	STERLING, RITA	Data Processing Information Center	Funct.
44	STERLING, RITA	Entry-Level Computer Programming	Funct.

DIRECTLY EXPERIENCED INDEX

Career Progression through Pursuit of Continuing Areas of Interest

			Level of Resp.
1	MURPHY	Field Sales	Mid
2	FOURNIER	Corporate Banking	Senior
3	LEHR	Financial Analyst	Mid
4	WILSON	Engineering Services/Telecommunications	Mid
5	CAPLAN	Human Services/Long-Term Facilities	Mid
6	JORDAN	Health Care Financial Services	Mid
7	NOLAN	Human Resources Management	Mid
8	LANGLEY	Operations Management	Senior
9	DELAHANTEE	Production Supervision: Assembly or Repair	Mid
10	CONRAD	Inspection Monitor/Quality Assurance	Mid
11	D'ORLANDO	Management: Purchasing and Materials Control	Senior
12	OLSON	Piping Supervisor/Large-Scale Construction Projects	Mid
13	LEWIS	Rn Charge Nurse/Long-Term Facility	Mid
14	KERRIGAN	Occupational Health Nurse	Mid
15	STUART	Accounting Services	Senior
16	ULLMAN	Marketing Professional	Mid
38	HANIFY	Product Support/Customer Service	Mid
41	PETRAS	Management Position/Admissions and Records	Mid

Career Renewal through Return to Earlier Areas of Interest

			Level of Resp.
17	HEALY	Marketing Services	Mid
37	HANIFY	Secondary School Teaching/Grades 7–12	Mid

CAREER-CHANGING INDEX

Launched Professionals Moving into New Areas

		From	To	Level of Resp.
18	MANCINI	Job Placement	Elder Services	Mid
22	KIRN	Corporate Accounting	Portfolio Management	Mid
23	RESTON	Manufacturing	Field Sales/Golf Products	Entry
24	THAYER	Dietetics	Sales of Nutritional Products	Entry
25	MALDEN	Educational Administration	Sales and Marketing	Entry
28	JANNELL	Retail Management	Financial Planning	Entry
30	KENNEDY	Claims Adjustment	Risk Management Services	Mid
31	HOLLAND	Risk Management	Telecommunications Consulting	Mid
32	JARDIN	Military Career	Civilian Administrative Mngmt.	Mid
34	FLEMING	Accounting	Human Resources/Employment	Entry
39	BUCKLEY	Customer Service	Technical Training	Mid
40	BUCKLEY	Customer Service	Employment Counseling	Mid
42	PETRAS	Admissions and Records	Public Accounting	Entry
43	STERLING	Foreign Language Education	DP Information Center Services	Entry
44	STERLING	Foreign Language Education	Computer Programming	Entry

Support Staff Moving into Entry Level Professional Positions

19	CONCANNON	Cashiering	Corporate Day Care Services	Entry
20	TAEGER	Administrative Support	Customer Service	Entry
21	KEEGAN	Theater Operations	Broadcast Media	Entry
26	KALE	Cashiering	Marketing Internship	Entry
27	KELLIHER	Administrative Support	Advertising	Entry
29	REILLY	Bartending	Public Accounting	Entry
33	PARADI	Collections	Paralegal Support Services	Entry
35	CORBETT	Legal Secretarial	Travel & Tourism Marketing Support	Entry
36	CORBETT	Legal Secretarial	Writing and Editing	Entry

CONTRIBUTING ROLE INDEX

PRODUCTION

Production Operations

Materials Management

MARKETING SERVICES

Research, Planning, Promotions, Product Management

Sales

Customer Service/Support

FINANCIAL SERVICES

Finance

Accounting

MANAGEMENT SUPPORT: PROFESSIONAL ADVISORY SERVICES

Administration

32	JARDIN	Administrative Management

Human Resources

7	NOLAN	Human Resources Management
34	FLEMING	Human Resources/Employment Services

MANAGEMENT SUPPORT: TECHNICAL ADVISORY SERVICES

Information Systems

39	BUCKLEY	Technical Training/HR Software Packages
43	STERLING	Data Processing Information Center
44	STERLING	Entry Level Computer Programming

Telecommunications

4	WILSON	Engineering Services/Telecommunications
31	HOLLAND	Telecommunications Management Consulting

EDUCATION

19	CONCANNON	Corporate Day Care Services
37	HANIFY	Secondary School Teaching/Grades 7–12
41	PETRAS	Management Position/Admissions and Records

HEALTH CARE

6	JORDAN	Health Care Financial Services
14	KERRIGAN	Occupational Health Nurse
13	LEWIS	RN Charge Nurse: Long-Term Facility

HUMAN SERVICES

5	CAPLAN	Human Services/Long-Term Facility
18	MANCINI	Elder Services
40	BUCKLEY	Employment Counselor

OTHER

12	OLSON	Piping Supervisor/Large-Scale Construction
21	KEEGAN	Broadcast Media
33	PARADI	Paralegal Support Services

JOSEPH MURPHY

Telephone:
(203) 678-2036

76 Whitman Lane
Farmington, CT 06032

OBJECTIVE

FIELD SALES

- Active Product Promotion   • New Business Development   • Strong Customer Service

QUALIFIED BY

Two years of professional experience in building and expanding a territory of five New England states with over 40 commercial accounts, and avocational pursuits involving strong teamwork and intense competition to achieve results. Open to significant travel.

KEY SKILLS

Account Development

- Prospecting • Cold Calling • Consultation • Presentation • Negotiation • Closing

Account Management

- Coordinating • Tracking • Checking • Expediting • Trouble-Shooting • Problem-Solving

EXPERIENCE

Directly Related Career Position:

SALES REPRESENTATIVE. Primo Inks, Inc., Waterbury, CT   (1991-Present)

- Sold diversified lines of ink to a broad customer base. Developed regional territory virtually from scratch, accessing business owners and key managers on the road, and at trade shows to stimulate interest and commitment to purchase supplies.
- Handled sales challenge of higher-end prices by development of positive rapport, solid product knowledge, motivating to buy quality, and a "service plus" attitude in meeting customer needs.
- Recently named Achievement Award Winner for most increased sales.

Part-Time Positions during College:

Operations Assistant; Corporate Driver. Montano Enterprises, Inc., Manchester, CT   (1986-1990)

- Analyzed years to date sales and payroll percentages for 32 retail stores and calculated percentages of loss prevention dollars per store.
- Assisted in upgrading of computer system for state-of-the-art graphics applications, and played key role in follow-up staff training.
- Earned special commendation for report formatting innovations resulting in more comprehensive and compact profiles of data.

EDUCATION

B.S. MANAGEMENT, 1991. University of Connecticut, Storrs, CT

On Dean's List for two semesters, with broad-based coursework in:

- Marketing
- Accounting
- Managerial Finance
- Economics
- Business Law
- Business Statistics
- Data Processing
- Basic Programming

Extracurricular Activities: Varsity Hockey Team and Community Hockey League

LEE FOURNIER

H: (617) 337-8473
O: (617) 773-4154

44 Birch Lane
Weymouth, MA 02188

OBJECTIVE

MANAGER OF A CORPORATE BANKING FACILITY

QUALIFIED BY

• Ten years of directly related and diversified experience with a major bank in soliciting, analyzing, and structuring commercial banking services to a broad range of industries.

• Extensive background in commercial lending including asset-based financing, international services, and real estate construction, with managerial experience at the regional level.

EXPERIENCE

State Street Bank & Trust, Quincy, MA

VICE PRESIDENT/AREA MANAGER, Braintree Branch   (1990-Present)

Developed and implemented an area management concept for six branch offices with combined footings of $80M. Managed the overall administration and marketing functions of the area. Directly supervised a team of four commercial lending officers and managed a $30M commercial loan portfolio. Increased commercial loan totals by 15% in 1992.

ASSISTANT VICE PRESIDENT/MANAGER, Randolph Office   (1988-1989)

Managed an office designated as a commercial loan center. Developed marketing programs that increased commercial loan totals by 50 percent, primarily through the acquisition of asset-based credits. Improved the office's internal audit rating from substandard to above average.

CORPORATE BANKING OFFICER, Quincy Corporate Office   (1986-1988)

Contributed to the growth of a new corporate banking center through new business development and the structuring of credit proposals to companies with sales up to $100M. Strong emphasis in the high technology industry.

ASSISTANT MANAGER, Weymouth Office   (1983-1985)

Advanced to this position from the bank's management training program. Served as an account officer for a $7.5M accounts receivable line of credit. Branch was named Office of the Year for top sales production.

EDUCATION

GRADUATE CERTIFICATE, BANKING, 1990. New England Banking Institute, Boston, MA

MBA, FINANCE, 1989. Bentley College, Waltham, MA

BS, ECONOMICS AND MANAGEMENT, 1982. Boston College, Chestnut Hill, MA

MEMBERSHIP

American Finance Association

LESLIE LEHR

Telephone:
(515) 281-2962

266 Taber Street
Des Moines, IA 50306

OBJECTIVE

FINANCIAL ANALYST

QUALIFIED BY

- Specialized graduate studies in finance, pursued on merit scholarship - GPA: 3.8; and
- Five years of corporate experience using analytical, planning, organizational and computer skills to track financial activity, administer salary planning, and audit expense accounts.

EDUCATION

MBA, FINANCE, 1993. Drake University, Des Moines, IA

BS, MARKETING MANAGEMENT, 1987. University of Iowa, Iowa City, IA

EXPERIENCE

Lockheed Aircraft International, Fort Madison, IA

OPERATIONS ANALYST   (1991-Present)

Maintained divisional documentation required in FAA certification and administered timekeeping budgets and charge lines.

- Improved cost effectiveness of timekeeping budgets by 10% using daily analysis.
- Conducted computer and systems management training for staff members leading to a 7% productivity increase.
- Extensive use of Digital WT/78 System and IBM-PC, with good working knowledge of Lotus and other business software.

COMPENSATION ANALYST   (1989-1991)

Handled the administration and analysis of salary planning exercises and management fund transactions for a division staffing over 2,000 employees, and coordination of labor rate, lead ratio, and financial activity analysis.

- Generated cost effectiveness study for relocating personnel overseas.
- Computerized service allowances, salary adjustments, and totems for division.
- Tracked and audited the financial activity of expense accounts for 60 employees.
- Selected as Divisional Employee of the Quarter out of a field of 2,000 employees, and received the Pride in Excellence Award for role in project organization.

Younker's, Des Moines, IA

DEPARTMENT SALES MANAGER, Fountain Plaza Store   (1988)

Managed staff on sales techniques, departmental procedures, merchandising, and inventory control in one of the store's top revenue generating departments. Supervised 5-8 employees.

- Promoted to department manager from management trainee position in less than three weeks.
- Surpassed previous year's department sales and profits by expanding market penetration 8% during a recessional season.
- Exceeded interstore department sales figures on a constant and consistent basis.

VICTOR WILSON

Telephone:
(603) 889-4528

187 Bell Lane
Merrimack, NH 03054

OBJECTIVE

ENGINEERING SERVICES/TELECOMMUNICATIONS

- Seasoned, Practical Judgment on Complex Problems
- High Standards of Quality, Timeliness and Cost Control
- Resource Coordination for Customer Satisfaction

QUALIFIED BY

Fourteen years of increasingly responsible positions in telecommunications, involving hands-on knowledge of electronic and key telephone equipment systems, and diverse experience with inside and outside plant installation, service and repair for residential and commercial customers.

Able to work under conditions of heavy pressure and resolve crises with calmness, ingenuity and speed. Adapt to new work environments and challenges quickly and efficiently.

KEY SKILLS

• Investigating	• Estimating	• Consulting	• Problem-Solving	• Installation
• Assessing	• Planning	• Coordinating	• Expediting	• Repair

EXPERIENCE

Technical Solutions, Inc., Nashua, NH - Subcontractor.   (1987-Present)
  Northern Telephone: OSP and Escalating Engineering

- Volunteered for expanded and upgraded job responsibilities as an escalating engineer, providing for uninterrupted coverage of the function at point of unexpected staff turn-over. Respond to medical emergencies, presidential appeals, and complex initial service and service restoration problems with "can-do" attitude and relaxed composure.

- Work closely with numerous internal departments, including the business office, the advocate group, and engineering, construction, installation and repair, maintenance and estimate assignment departments to ensure reliable and smooth implementation of service orders.

- Ensured that crucial assignment dates for service to State Lottery Commission ticket machines at over 200 field sites were met on time, with error-free installation.

- Took on primary responsibility for completing an estimate in progress of a service rehab to an 1,800 residential customer area interrupted by a major work stoppage. Met due date with short staffing and in inclement weather conditions.

- Supervised a crew of 14 installers, providing orientation to geography and job function and overseeing completion of work orders to eliminate backlog of service requests.

United Telenet, Cincinnati, OH - Subcontractor.   (1984-1987)
  MCI and Ohio Bell: Installation and Maintenance

Network Connections, Burlington, MA - Partner.   (1982-1984)
  Gencom and AT &T: Installation and Programming

Teletech, Inc., Chelmsford, MA - Lab Supervisor.   (1979-1981)

EDUCATION

U.S. Army - Field Communications Training and Assignments
Society of Network Engineers - Extensive Continuing Education

CATHERINE CAPLAN

Telephone:
(606) 253-5246

77 Parker Road
Lexington, KY 40507

OBJECTIVE

HUMAN SERVICES/LONG-TERM FACILITIES

• Core Commitment to Resident Wellbeing   • Collaborative Teamwork for Quality Care

QUALIFIED BY

Nine years of intensive staff experience in non-profit organizations providing services to pervasively developmentally disabled clients, including two and a half years in supervision of instructional aides. Broad-based work in assisting in formulating, implementing and documenting treatment plans for autism, emotional disturbance, mental retardation and physical disabilities.

Strong belief in the uniqueness and potential of every person, however disabled. Patience, realism, resourcefulness, stamina and dedication in encouraging progress, learning and growth.

KEY SKILLS

• Observing • Assessing • Planning • Motivating • Training • Helping

• Living Skills Development • Behavioral Management • Crisis Intervention • Staff Supervision

EXPERIENCE

Lighthouse Services, Inc., Frankfort, KY
A residential school for 30 multi-handicapped adolescents.

SUBSTITUTE STAFFPERSON (1988-Present)

Assignments in shift supervision, teaching, instruction, classroom aid, and nurse's assistance.

INSTRUCTOR (1985-1988); and TEACHER'S ASSISTANT (1984-1985)

Supervised classroom of 6 medically and behaviorally involved students, and 2 full-time aides and 2-4 part-time aides. Kept close family contact. Developed and used Individual Educational Plans, progress reports and behavioral program. Used total communication systems for building socialization, cognitive, peer interaction, pre-voc and leisure time skills. Produced newsletter.

Morgan Place, Lexington, KY
A residential group home for eight autistic and emotionally disturbed adolescent males.

AWAKE OVERNIGHT COUNSELOR (1992); and PRIMARY COUNSELOR (1988-1992)

Ensured safety and wellbeing of all residents during overnight and morning, and kept daily logs. With three residents, assisted in all facets of personal living, led group and individual meetings, organized extensive recreational activities, and developed and implemented behavioral programs.

EDUCATION

Two years of full-time college coursework in general education and personal interest areas -
Antioch College, Yellow Springs, OH; and University of Kentucky, Lexington, KY
Continuing Education: Numerous seminars and conferences for Human Services Professionals

Involvement over 9 years with:
KY Approved Private Schools; Association for Retarded Citizens; and Child Care Workers

BRADLEY JORDAN

Telephone:
(913) 345-9687

352 Central Street
Overland Park, KS 66207

OBJECTIVE

HEALTH CARE FINANCIAL SERVICES

Cost Containment and Growth Strategies for Profitable Operations

QUALIFIED BY

Two years of professional experience in hospital finance with in-depth involvement in all aspects of third party payment transactions, backed by college degree and continuing education in health care management issues, trends and resources.

Management position in service business overseeing all administrative operations, with constant attunement to anticipating and satisfying customer needs.

EDUCATION

B.S. HEALTH CARE ADMINISTRATION, 1991. University of Kansas, Lawrence, KS

Professional Development: Advanced Reimbursement; and Health Care Finance for Accountants

KEY SKILLS

• Monitoring • Tracking • Analyzing • Planning • Communicating

EXPERIENCE

Ames Hospital, Kansas City, KS: REIMBURSEMENT & BUDGET ACCOUNTANT (1991-Present)

• Oversaw the maintenance of the Medicare log, ensuring the integrity and timeliness of over 300 entries per month and resolving all discrepancies in year-end audit. Commended by supervisor for key contribution to significant cost savings.

• Created numerous and varied Lotus 1-2-3 spreadsheets for tracking and analyzing statistical data, including two reports reviewed in monthly executive board meetings.

• Wrote ad hoc reports in Harmony, SMS to download into Lotus, resulting in a 25% time saving in preparation of third party projected contractual agreements and elimination of human error from previous non-automated process.

• Developed a slide show using Harvard Graphics demonstrating positive trends of hospital growth in a profiling of two fiscal years.

• Maintained active interdepartmental communications on a hospital-wide basis for a ready-reference statistical data base used in diverse financial reporting.

Zenith Fitness Club, Bonner Springs, KS: NIGHT MANAGER (1988-1990; 1992-Present)

• Optimized club use for maximal earnings. Carefully monitored facility maintenance needs and services. Maintained a high level of customer satisfaction with a broad business membership.

PROFESSIONAL AFFILIATIONS

Healthcare Financial Management Association

American Hospital Association

DAVID NOLAN

H: (914) 761-7416
O: (212) 807-0671

64 Glenellen Road
White Plains, NY 10606

OBJECTIVE

HUMAN RESOURCES MANAGEMENT

QUALIFIED BY

Sixteen years of increasingly responsible personnel management experience, with skills in:

MANAGEMENT AND ADMINISTRATION

- Organization Planning
- Work Force Utilization
- Personnel Systems/HRIS
- Security/Safety Administration

RECRUITING AND STAFFING

- Direct Recruiting
- Agency Liaison & Administration
- College Relations
- Recruiting Advertising

EMPLOYEE RELATIONS

- EEO/AA Administration
- Employee Assistance Programs
- Employee Communications

LABOR RELATIONS

- Contract Administration
- Bargaining/Negotiations
- Grievance Handling

TRAINING AND DEVELOPMENT

- Team Building Processes
- Total Quality Management
- Career Development/Succession

COMPENSATION AND BENEFITS

- Salary Planning/Administration
- Incentive/Performance Systems
- Benefits Administration

EXPERIENCE

HUMAN RESOURCES MANAGER, General Instruments Corp., New York, NY   (1987-Present)

Reporting to the Vice President, responsible for all H.R. activities in the Eastern Division.

Examples of accomplishments include a 13% reduction of attrition, initiation of team training, innovative compensation program and policy revisions, introduction of TQM processes, and establishment of an open door policy to resolve personnel issues and employee complaints.

STAFF PERSONNEL ADMINISTRATOR, Grumman Corp., Bethpage, NY   (1982-1986)

Directed recruitment for scientists, engineers, programmers, managers and others in support of commercial and military programs. Led corporate recruitment teams at staffing centers and job fairs throughout the United States. Implemented international recruitment programs.

Examples of accomplishments included a 30% reduction in cost per hire through direct sourcing, cost and quality improvement by managing recruiting ads, and design of training in administrative practices.

PERSONNEL MANAGER, New York Times Co., New York, NY   (1977-1982)

Managed all personnel activities involving a 2,000 employee distribution company.

Examples of accomplishments included development of employee enrichment programs which significantly increased morale and reduced grievances, development of a competitive in industry compensation program, development of an EEO response which improved community relations and allayed complaints, and an incrementally implemented-cost effective-benefits program.

EDUCATION

INDUSTRIAL RELATIONS, 30 Graduate Units. Columbia University, New York, NY
BS, BUSINESS ADMINISTRATION, 1976. Cornell University, Ithaca, NY

CHESTER LANGLEY

H: (617) 575-6943
O: (617) 227-2657

366 Magnolia Drive
Canton, MA 02021

OBJECTIVE

OPERATIONS MANAGEMENT

QUALIFIED BY

Sixteen years of increasingly responsible management experience using planning, decision-making, problem-solving, motivational and financial skills to oversee safe, efficient and cost-effective manufacturing operations, backed by specialized business and technical degrees.

AREAS OF EFFECTIVENESS

- Strategic Planning
- Capital & Operational Budgeting
- Financial Analysis & Cost Control
- Production & Inventory Management

- Technical Operations Analysis
- Regulatory Compliance
- Human Resource Management
- Customer Service

EXPERIENCE

Typro, Aerospace and Industrial Adhesives, a Division of the Baxter Corporation

DIRECTOR OF OPERATIONS	Boston, MA	(1989-Present)

Whittier Industrial

VICE PRESIDENT OF OPERATIONS	Chelsea, MA	(1987-1988)

Monsanto Co.

PLANT MANAGER	Springfield, MA	(1986)
ASSISTANT TO PLANT MANAGER	Liverpool, England	(1985)
PRODUCTION SUPERINTENDENT	Springfield, MA	(1981-1984)
PLANT START-UP LIAISON	Liverpool, England	(1979-1981)
PRODUCTION SUPERINTENDENT	Everett, MA	(1977-1978)

EDUCATION

MBA, FINANCE, 1989. Babson College, Wellesley, MA

BS, CHEMICAL ENGINEERING, 1976. University of Lowell, Lowell, MA

CHESTER LANGLEY

RELATED ACCOMPLISHMENTS

For **Typro**, a Manufacturer of High Tech Specialty Adhesives -
A job shop operation with 7 year lead time on new product acceptance.
Quality performance and customer service are crucial.

- Managed customer service department, with goal of gaining greater market share from larger adhesive manufacturers through better technical service and product delivery than competition.

- Prepared $5 million operating budget. Maintained production requirements within budget. Budgeted future capital equipment needs and developed justification for their purpose.

- Negotiated purchasing contracts of up to $1 million with major vendors to achieve cost reductions. Raw materials are 80% of total cost of goods sold.

- Directed production scheduling and inventory control. Meeting production schedule without accumulation of excess inventory of raw material, intermediates, or finished goods is critical. Achieved 35% raw material consignment to reduce inventory carry costs.

- Managed production of high quality specialty adhesives ($20+ million sales). Majority of products are made to order. Conformity to rigid customer specifications is an absolute requirement. Operating within regulatory guidelines is met or exceeded.

For **Whittier Industrial**, a Small, Closely Held Hazardous Waste Company -
Service area: Eastern MA.
Price competition and immediate responsiveness were keys to success.

- Managed a major waste transportation company with 35 trucks, 150 unionized employees and 600 customers. Negotiated and administered union contracts, ensured governmental compliance, resolved customer concerns, and performed net present value analysis of projects.

For **Monsanto Co.**, a Heavy Industrial and Agricultural Chemical Manufacturer -
Main profit centers were selective commodity and agricultural chemicals.
Cost control and on-time delivery were critical management factors.

- Directed chemical plant operations manufacturing 20+ products and employing 120 unionized employees on environmentally sensitive coast. Prepared, submitted and operated within $6 million annual budget, and arranged production and turn-arounds to meet sales.

- Determined process bottlenecks in three production units. Instituted process modifications that increased production by 20% and reduced labor and raw material costs by 30%.

- Handled chemical crisis in which 52 citizens were hospitalized. Met with media and responded to their questions and worked with public agencies to initiate methods to prevent recurrence.

- Instituted new employee safety program that reduced accident rate by 50%.

- Negotiated 3 union contracts. Resolved 81 day work stoppage while obtaining management job combination goals. Maintained high morale, and broke most previous production records.

MEMBERSHIP

American Association of Industrial Management

ROY DELAHANTEE

Telephone:
(313) 291-4054

214 Parkdale Street
Taylor, MI 48180

OBJECTIVE

PRODUCTION SUPERVISION: ASSEMBLY OR REPAIR

QUALIFIED BY

- Twenty plus years of increasingly responsible experience in related areas of assembly and repair, with fourteen years in supervisory positions;

- Well-developed strengths in working with and through other people, trouble-shooting practical problems, and generating and implementing innovative solutions.

AREAS OF EFFECTIVENESS

- Assembly & Repair Knowledge
- Quality Assurance
- Modelling, Coaching & OJT
- Cost Savings & Control

RELATED ACCOMPLISHMENTS

In Production Operations of a Fortune 500 Company:

- Supervised a crew of 12 repairpersons - one in water-test, one in glass, two in soft trim, and eight in hard trim. Assessed capabilities of crew, tailoring assignments to varying ability levels, and building pride in productivity and a shared sense of teamwork. Closely approached World Class Quality, with only three defects in daily audit year, providing ready-to-deliver cars for customer satisfaction.

- Faced a ground system problem requiring repair in over 1,000 cars. Used a participative management approach to generate ideas while remaining sensitive to labor relations issues felt by crew members. Solution identified and implemented led to more repairs accomplished on the night shift in one hour than the day shift accomplished in eight hours.

- Assessed untapped potential for repair of previously scrapped major parts, such as malfunctioning steering columns. Trained a high potential person to trouble-shoot designated problem areas, while stimulating desire to learn and initiative in other members of the repair crew. Result: replacement of a 25¢ horn cam or a $20 harness versus a $200 steering column.

- Devised idea and delegated developing that idea for a more effective method for replacing defective shift cables, significantly simplifying the task to expedite results, and increasing individual job satisfaction and cost savings to the company.

- Served as one of three production supervisors coordinating the implementation of Department 17 painting, overseeing 170 people in general painting and precision marking for hazardous material, fire lanes and general traffic through the plant. Received merit award for excellence.

EXPERIENCE

Supervisor of Repair (1984-1992); Supervisor of Assembly (1978-1983); Hourly (1970-1978).
Chrysler Corporation, Highland Park, MI

EDUCATION

BS, BUSINESS MANAGEMENT, 1978. Detroit College of Business, Dearborn, MI

STEVEN CONRAD

Telephone:
(503) 373-2106

128 Minton Street
Salem, OR 97310

OBJECTIVE

INSPECTION MONITOR/QUALITY ASSURANCE

QUALIFIED BY

- Fourteen years of direct experience in monitoring production processes and materials for conformity to specifications, with reputation for precision and reliability.

- Well-developed observational skills, with commitment to careful checking of details to support product quality, and fast action on identified problems.

KEY SKILLS

- Inspection   • Testing   • Reporting   • Training

RELATED ACCOMPLISHMENTS

- Organized workload of hourly inspectors to eliminate unnecessary travel about the plant and redundancy of effort, and assure fair distribution of labor.

- Set up testing of welding repair staff to assess capability in fusion welding, and arrange for training as needed, to reduce unnecessary repairs and support a quality product from the outset.

- Served as the primary provider in Quality Assurance of SPC on torque of critical fasteners, bringing enhanced ability to pinpoint faulty parts, failing tools, and ineffective areas of production processes.

- Set up a labor-effective approach to destructive weld-testing, introducing hydraulic equipment to shorten the time necessary to determine strength of fusion.

- Designed a worksheet for verification of computer-controlled torque in Inspection Department to facilitate quick identification of discrepancies in production operations and corrective action.

- Provided decision-making support to Quality Assurance management, for example, evaluating resources for improved data collection such as the new GSE Data-Stat.

EXPERIENCE

INSPECTOR, QUALITY ASSURANCE. Freightliner Corp., Portland, OR (1979-Present)

EDUCATION

SCIENCE TECHNOLOGIES - 45 Units. Oregon Institute of Technology, Klamath Falls, OR

Employer-Sponsored Training:

- Total Quality Management
- Teamwork for Excellence
- Project Management
- Computer Aided Manufacturing
- Problem-Solving/Decision-Making
- Material Requirements Planning

JAMES D'ORLANDO

Telephone:
(302) 734-3982

346 Bellaire Road
Dover, DE 19903

OBJECTIVE

UPPER MANAGEMENT: PURCHASING AND/OR MATERIALS CONTROL

QUALIFIED BY

• Sixteen years of supervisory experience in allied areas of materials management;

• Leadership in state-of-the-art technology for more efficient and cost-effective operations; and

• Thriving on challenges posed by change, perseverance in problem-solving, and ease in working with diverse kinds of people.

EXPERIENCE

Du Pont, Wilmington, DE

SUPERVISOR, GENERAL STORES & PURCHASING	(1983-Present)
SUPERVISOR, MATERIAL CONTROL	(1977-1982)
RELATED SUPPORT POSITIONS	(1968-1976)

AREAS OF EFFECTIVENESS

• Logistics Management   • Human Relations

RELATED ACCOMPLISHMENTS

• Adapted corporate-wide general stores and purchasing program - Olympic Computer System - for Wilmington facility, and coordinated implementation successfully, including training of hourly personnel. Oversaw team representing Engineering, EDS, Accounting and Purchasing to factor in complex technical and business issues posed by the system. Impact: significant cost savings and reduction of unnecessary inventory by 20%.

• Reduced staffing in General Stores from eight to five positions by assessing work loads in departmental operations and consolidating functions.

• Established Eastern regional purchasing area serving five locations, defining steel, electrical and plumbing supplies needed, soliciting and evaluating bids, and making final purchasing decisions. Realized savings of 10% and better through joint price negotiations.

• Established a track record of problem-free labor-management relations by respecting viewpoints of employees and receiving respect in return. Results: virtually no grievances filed in eleven years, with high level of morale and productivity in departmental employees.

EDUCATION

BS, MANAGEMENT. University of Delaware, Newark, DE

MEMBERSHIP

National Association of Purchasing Management

FRANK OLSON

Telephone:
(703) 620-2939

54 Willow Glen Road
Reston, VA 22091

OBJECTIVE

PIPING SUPERVISOR / LARGE-SCALE CONSTRUCTION PROJECTS

QUALIFIED BY

Sixteen years of increasingly responsible experience in all facets of piping construction. Domestic and international project assignments with multi-national companies. Seasoned judgment, resourceful and flexible.

Key Skills: Assessing, Advising, Trouble-Shooting, Problem-Solving and Improvising.

AREAS OF EFFECTIVENESS

• WORK CREW SUPERVISION
• DRAWING INTERPRETATION • ISOMETRICS • FABRICATION • ERECTION
• QUALITY CONTROL AND LIAISON WITH INSPECTORS

PROFESSIONAL EDUCATION AND TRAINING

LICENSED SPRINKLER JOURNEYMAN, State of Virginia
FIRE SPRINKLER SYSTEMS DESIGN, Virginia Polytechnic Institute, Blacksburg, VA

CERTIFICATES, WELDER'S TEST, ASME IX:
Baker Testing Services, Arlington, VA; and Metlab International Ltd., London

NATIONAL CRAFT CERTIFICATE, MECHANICAL FITTING, 1979
Department of Education/Training and Employment Authority, England

Course and Field Work Concentrations in:
• Fitters Work • Turners Work • Engineering Workshop Theory • Technical Drawing

DIPLOMA, King's Row Technical School, Liverpool, England
 Math, Science, Metalwork, and Drafting

EXPERIENCE

PIPEFITTER/WELDER, Utility Construction Corp., Alexandria, VA   (1989-Present)

SUBCONTRACTOR, DIVERSE PIPING PROJECTS, London, England:

Prime Developers	(1988)	Elgin International Ltd.	(1983)
Industrial Building	(1987-1988)	Alden, Winslow & Rowe	(1982-1983)
J. Murphy & Sons	(1986)	Thomas & Sons, Inc.	(1980-1981)
A.E. Engineering Co.	(1984-1985)	J.B.D. Construction, Ltd.	(1977-1980)

IN-DEPTH INVOLVEMENT WITH:

• Off-Shore Platform Construction
• High Pressure Natural Gas Pipelines and Pressure-Reducing Stations
• Chemical, Pharmaceutical, and Food Plants
• Power Stations • Oil Refineries • Petroleum Tank Farms • Boiler Construction

• Key field supervison in charge of turn-key operations for a variety of mechanical engineering companies, consistently meeting stringent time schedules and completing high quality work within budget.

• Crew direction with up to eight pipefitters and welders on high precision work, assigning work to capitalize on individual expertise, and teaming up workers to realize their best potential.

• Engineering coordination on piping modifications, advising on feasibility, executing complex technical changes, and documenting same for adjusted billing of client companies.

MARJORY LEWIS

Telephone:
(617) 383-2497

189 Foster Road
Cohasset, MA 02025

OBJECTIVE

RN CHARGE NURSE
LONG-TERM FACILITY: RESIDENTIAL OR ADULT DAY CARE

• Dedicated Direct Care • Collaborative Teamwork • Sensitive Family Relations

QUALIFIED BY

Specialized training and direct professional experience attending to the health care needs of the elderly, early career foundations in general nursing services, non-clinical employment emphasizing timely and responsive customer service, and homemaking and community involvement activities demonstrating calmness, conscientiousness, responsibility, seasoned judgment, and patience.

EXPERIENCE

Health Care Positions:

STAFF NURSE per diem, Connors Elder Care, Hingham, MA	(1992-Present)
STAFF NURSE/CLINICAL PRACTICUM, Geri-Support Services, Quincy, MA	(1991)
INSTRUCTOR, Edwards Hospital School of Nursing, Concord, MA	(1964-1967)
STAFF NURSE, Massachusetts General Hospital, Boston, MA	(1960-1963)

Other Professional Employment:

Office Manager/Customer Service Rep, Sullivan Insurance Services, Scituate, MA	(1988-1991)

EDUCATION AND LICENSURE

CERTIFICATE, WHOLISTIC CARE FOR THE ELDERLY, 1991, Simmons College, Boston, MA
BSN, Northeastern University. DIPLOMA, NURSING, Faulkner Hospital, Jamaica Plain, MA

REGISTERED NURSE, State of MA - Maintained consistently since entry into profession.

KEY SKILLS

• Observing • Monitoring • Organizing • Listening • Documenting • Prioritizing • Follow-Up

RELATED ACCOMPLISHMENTS

In medium-sized skilled nursing facilities:

• Worked closely with interdisciplinary team, including physicians, LPNs and nursing assistants, dieticians, physical therapists, and social service professionals to monitor, maintain and enhance the wellbeing of residents with a wide variety of physical illnesses and limitations.

• Completed MDSs and formulated nursing care plans closely tailored to individual needs, with careful review and revision on a regular basis.

• Supervised direct nursing care to chronically ill residents, and ensured observation of stringent hygiene and safety standards. As well, coordinated with other nurses and housekeeping and maintenance staff on meeting equipment and supply needs.

• Dispensed medication and administered treatments for numerous and varied serious health problems such as strokes, cardiac and pulmonary disease, and Alzheimer's.

In professional service-provider offices where active concern for customer needs, accurate record-keeping and fast follow-up were essential to attracting and retaining business:

• Provided counsel on insurance coverage and expedited processing of claims, working as liaison with both customers and providers, and administered smooth-running office operations.

ALANA KERRIGAN

Telephone:
(314) 889-4416

14 Grace Road
St. Louis, MO 63105

OBJECTIVE

OCCUPATIONAL HEALTH NURSE

Consultation, Education and Treatment for Wellness in the Workplace

QUALIFIED BY

Twenty years of diverse experience in nursing, including eight years in occupational health. Commitment to quality patient care, calmness in emergencies, and clarity and caring in communications with employees, management and outside vendors. Accuracy, promptness and efficiency in attending to related administrative functions.

EXPERIENCE

Directly Related Employment:

OCCUPATIONAL HEALTH NURSE, General Dynamics Corp., St. Louis, MO   (1985-1993)

Other Professional Employment:

ON-CALL NURSE, Med Staff, Clayton, MO (1981-1984)
NURSING SUPERVISOR, Corning Clinic, Jennings, MO (1975-1980)
STAFF NURSE, Thompson Hospital, St. Louis, MO (1973-1974)

AREAS OF EFFECTIVENESS

• Direct Nursing Care   • Health Counseling   • Information and Referral
• Employee Evaluation and Job Assignment   • Records Management and Payment Processing

RELATED ACCOMPLISHMENTS

• Averaged 65-100 patient visits per day in services directly benefitting individual employees and overall plant operations. Conducted diagnostic hearing tests, blood tests, X-Rays, and EKGs. Treated minor occupational injuries such as lacerations, sprains, strains, burns and eye problems, and occupationally related illnesses. Provided on-site physical therapy.

• Provided a listening ear, emotional support and linkage to appropriate internal and community resources for employees with personal and family problems and alcohol and drug dependency. Impact: support of on-the-job productivity and reduction of absenteeism and turn-over costs.

• Evaluated employees in numerous and varied job classifications for necessary work restrictions and availability for assignments. Gained management support for temporary and permanent reassignments. Impact: minimizing lost time from work, and Workman's Comp savings.

• Maintained accurate, up-to-date records for over 1,500 employees, including current problems and health histories of employees returning to work from medical leaves.

• Made initial payment approvals for employee medical bills from doctors, hospitals and numerous other service-providers. Processed as many as 20 forms in a shift while juggling direct provision of care, and regularly meeting timelines requested for expedited payments.

• Generated significant savings on departmental treatment equipment by demonstrating purchase advantage over rental costs regularly incurred. Received Suggestion Award recognition.

EDUCATION

BSN, 1984. Webster University, St. Louis, MO. RN, 1972. Jackson Hospital, St Louis, MO

GENE STUART

Telephone:
(303) 279-1877

6 Woodland Way
Golden, CO 80401

OBJECTIVE

ACCOUNTING SERVICES

Management or Senior Professional Staff Position

QUALIFIED BY

Eighteen years of direct and diversified experience involving staff and management responsibility for the preparation, accuracy, reporting, and audit and regulatory compliance of accounting and tax data, supported by specialized education in business and accounting.

KEY SKILLS

Performance of responsibilities with limited supervision as a dedicated, stable member of the accounting team providing:

- Liaison
- Design
- Analysis
- Standardization
- Problem-Solving
- Staff Training

AREAS OF EFFECTIVENESS

- Reconciliaton of Books and Records
- Accounting Systems and Management Reports
- Audit and Regulatory Compliance
- Budget Planning and Monitoring
- Accurate Preparation of Complex Tax Returns
- Property Development and Sales Accounting

RELATED ACCOMPLISHMENTS

In employment by Savings and Loan Associations with assets from $100 Million to over $2 Billion and involving Related, Subsidiary and Parent Corporations:

- Served as liaison and chief accountant, established a functioning accounting department, balanced accounts and records, prepared management and regulatory reports, and financial documents necessary for the sale of a related association that resulted in an after-tax profit in excess of $1 Million.

- Served as liaison to independent audit and regulatory examination personnel, maintaining open channels of communication and providing the data necessary for the completion of their tasks.

- Prepared and supervised the preparation of federal, consolidated corporate federal, state, combined unitary state, property, and business tax returns ranging up to income in excess of $100 Million.

GENE STUART

RELATED ACCOMPLISHMENTS (continued)

- Handled the audit and examination of federal and state tax returns that resulted in no surprise assessments and the acceptance of several controversial tax treatments involving several million dollars.

- Prepared and monitored budgets for development projects with costs ranging to $30 Million, and utilized the budgets to compute project profits that met the requirements of audit, regulatory and tax personnel.

- Designed and maintained the accounting and reporting systems for real estate projects constructed and sold over a period of several years, involving multiple owners and investors and comprised of hundreds of individual units with multiple problems.

- Performed duties and projects required during times of business turmoil and change, maintaining the respect and loyalty of staff members through assistance and training.

EXPERIENCE

Aurora Savings Bank, Aurora, CO

VICE PRESIDENT, SECONDARY MARKETING	(1991-1993)
SENIOR VICE PRESIDENT OF FINANCE	(1989-1990)
VICE PRESIDENT, CONTROLLER	(1988-1989)

Lakewood Savings Bank, Lakewood, CO

VICE PRESIDENT, MANAGEMENT INFORMATION	(1980-1988)
ACCOUNTING OPERATIONS COORDINATOR	(1978-1980)

Ernst & Whinney, Denver, CO

SENIOR AUDITOR	(1977)
STAFF AUDITOR	(1975-1977)
SUMMER INTERN	(1974)

EDUCATION

BS, ACCOUNTING, with Honors, 1974. University of Denver, Denver, CO

Numerous Professional Development Seminars in Auditing, Accounting and Corporate Taxation

Licensing: Active Certified Public Accountant

MEMBERSHIP

National Society of Public Accountants

TERI ULLMAN

H: (301) 266-1627
O: (301) 539-3035

32 Amber Drive
Annapolis, MD 21041

OBJECTIVE

MARKETING PROFESSIONAL

QUALIFIED BY

Specialized business studies, and four years of directly related, diversified, and increasingly responsible work experience in developing marketing strategy, and conducting and managing campaigns for corporate communications and product promotion.

KEY SKILLS

• Consultation • Decision-Making • Coordinating • Trouble-Shooting • Problem-Solving

AREAS OF EFFECTIVENESS

• Strategic Marketing Plans

• Promotional Materials and Events

• Supervision, Team-Building and Internal Administration

RELATED ACCOMPLISHMENTS

For a public relations firm billing $300K+ per year, with a broad spectrum of clients including real estate, financial, high tech, and consumer product firms:

• Generated 3-12 month, integrated marketing/public relations plans focusing on media placement, the development of marketing collaterals, and special event promotion.

• Developed and placed news releases, feature stories, and public service announcements resulting in maximum exposure of 150 news clippings per month on a local/regional/national level, while account supervisor on a new product introduction campaign.

• Targeted interviews for clients with print and broadcast media and acted as media spokesperson.

• Coordinated the development of marketing collaterals, including corporate newsletters and brochures, from overseeing logo and format design to ensuring quality photography and copy.

• Organized regional press conferences with national exposure resulting in placement in national magazines like *Newsweek, Businessweek,* and *Venture;* in major metropolitan newspapers like *USA Today,* the *Los Angeles Times,* and the *Chicago Sun;* and on national television and radio networks including CBS and ABC.

TERI ULLMAN   Page Two

RELATED ACCOMPLISHMENTS (continued)

- Planned the catering, set design, and marketing for 10 real estate broker open houses to promote client properties, with an attendance of 200+ each.

- Interviewed, and helped select, train and develop account executives, summer interns, an office support staff, and all outside vendors.

- Supervised internal operations and assessed output through annual reviews within a six person public relations office.

- Managed and coordinated all aspects of commercial accounts receivables and accounts payables.

EXPERIENCE

CAREER POSITIONS:

Employment -

GENERAL MANAGER/ACCOUNTS SUPERVISOR   (1991-Present)
ACCOUNT EXECUTIVE   (1989-1991)

    Smith and Chandler, Woodmoor, MD

Professional Group Leadership -

LOCAL CHAPTER PRESIDENT   (1992)

    Maryland Federation of Business and Professional Women
    Selected as the Young Careerist of the Year for the largest MD district.

OTHER BUSINESS BACKGROUND:

CLAIMS ANALYST   (1986-1988)

    Commercial Credit Corp., Baltimore, MD

EDUCATION

BS ECONOMICS, Summa Cum Laude, 1985. The Johns Hopkins University, Baltimore, MD

MEMBERSHIPS

American Marketing Association
Public Relations Society of America

ANDI HEALY

Telephone:
(504) 834-4722

142 Hawthorne Drive
Metairie, LA 70005

OBJECTIVE

MARKETING SERVICES

Consumer Research and Analysis
Marketing Strategies
Product Management
Sales Promotion

QUALIFIED BY

Specialized preparation at the graduate level in business management and marketing,
and 18 years of diverse work experience developing and implementing marketing objectives,
meeting deadlines, and working in collaborative teams to assess and meet client needs.

KEY SKILLS

- Analyzing   • Planning   • Decision-Making

- Coordinating   • Problem-Solving   • Trouble-Shooting   • Expediting   • Monitoring

RELATED ACCOMPLISHMENTS

For an independent optometrist providing eyecare services and products:

- Collaborated in marketing plan development, of long-term strategies and short-term objectives.

- Supervised design of office space for functionality, visual impact and comfort.

- Developed and edited promotional materials used in successful business development campaign.

- Analyzed office production and trouble-shot problems in client services.

For advertising agencies operating on a regional and local level:

- Coordinated public relations for clients in a wide range of small and mid-size businesses.

- Developed advertising media budgets, coordinated media and creative productions,
  and produced camera-ready artwork and lay-outs for production.

For retail stores and specialty service providers:

- Offered multi-faceted services to attract and serve clothing customers, including advertising
  copy-writing, fashion show coordination, merchandising displays and sales promotion.

For a local school district:

- Coordinated multi-disciplinary team to assess target population needs.

- Researched relevant resources, and developed, delivered and evaluated customized programs.

- Generated in-house communications for professional staff, and coordinated public relations
  aimed at referral sources for special services.

ANDI HEALY

EXPERIENCE

Related Employment in Business:

OFFICE MANAGER/MARKETING CONSULTANT

    Dr. Richard Healy, Kenner, LA   (1980-Present)

ADVERTISING MEDIA & PRODUCTION

Price, Phillips and Webster, Inc., St. Charles, LA	(1978-1979)
Evans Advertising, Chalmette, LA	(1976-1978)
New Orleans Business, Gretna, LA	(1976)

SALES REPRESENTATIVE

D.H. Holmes College Board, New Orleans, LA	(1975)
Simplicity Fashions, La Place, LA	(1975)

Other Professional Employment:

EDUCATOR/PROGRAM ADMINISTRATOR

    New Orleans School System, New Orleans, LA   (1980-Present)

EDUCATION

MBA, MARKETING - In Progress. University of New Orleans, New Orleans, LA

MS, EDUCATION, 1980. Tulane University, New Orleans, LA

BA, ENGLISH, 1975. Rice University, Houston, TX

Coursework Relevant to Objective:

- Marketing for Managers
- Marketing Planning
- Marketing Management
- Consumer Behavior
- Advertising Strategies
- Graphic Design
- Journalism Fundamentals
- Magazine & Newsletter Writing

MEMBERSHIPS

American Marketing Association

Admark Advertising and Marketing Association

BONNIE MANCINI

Telephone:
(617) 786-8546

367 Cameron Road
Quincy, MA 02169

OBJECTIVE

ELDER SERVICES

- Wellness and Recreation Programs
- Talent Recruitment for Community Service
- Practical Problem-Solving Assistance
- Support Systems for Crisis Management

QUALIFIED BY

A long-standing track record of leadership and service in a wide variety of community groups, and over a decade of professional work experience in public sector and non-profit organizations. Demonstrated strengths in creative program development, mobilizing resources, working in a team, and supervising volunteers.

KEY SKILLS

- Assessing
- Planning
- Organizing
- Coordinating
- Publicizing
- Promoting
- Advising
- Facilitating

EXPERIENCE

Contributed Services:

BOARD MEMBER - Two Years Each with:
Quincy Housing Partnership; Quincy Coalition for the Homeless; and St. Ann's Service Corps

Extensive Prior Involvement:

VOLUNTEER, Boston Food Bank; Pine Street Inn; Mary's Place; The Grange; & UNESCO.
CO-FOUNDER, South Shore Council for Intercultural Exchange, Boston, MA
CO-FOUNDER, Agathan Women's Club, St. Agatha's Church, Milton, MA
BOARD MEMBER and SENIOR LEADER, Campfire Girls, USA, Boston, MA

Employment:

JOB COUNSELOR, MA Department of Employment & Training, Quincy, MA   (1974-1982)

> Provided employment counseling and job placement services to a wide range of clients including housewives, blue collar workers and white collar professionals. As well, assisted with information and referral as needed to over 25 public agencies.

GUIDANCE COUNSELOR, Quincy Junior High School, Quincy, MA   (1970-1972)

> Offered individual and group counseling and crisis intervention assistance to a caseload of over 340 students. Edited a newsletter spotlighting special programs and volunteers, served as advisor to the Red Cross Club, and formed a Community Service Club involving over one third of the student body.

EXECUTIVE DIRECTOR, Campfire Girls USA, Boston, MA   (1969)

> Managed office and programs supporting over 300 volunteer troop leaders, served as liaison with community groups, and supervised overnight and day camp operations and trips.

EDUCATION

MS, COUNSELING.   Boston College, Chestnut Hill, MA

BA, GOVERNMENT. Simmons College, Boston, MA

ANNA CONCANNON

Telephone:
(414) 656-9766

246 Cherry Street
Kenosha, WI 53141

OBJECTIVE

CORPORATE DAY CARE SERVICES

• Innovative Strategies for Learning and Play   • Attentive, Affectionate and Flexible Supervision

QUALIFIED BY

Four years of diversified experience in caring for infants and pre-school children, backed by directly relevant college studies. Ability to set standards and boundaries while creating a warm, lively and fun environment for personal growth. Enthusiastic, patient, steady and calm in anticipating and responding to multi-level needs. Safety-conscious, careful and responsible.

KEY SKILLS

• Observing • Listening • Leading • Motivating • Entertaining • Instructing • Helping

EXPERIENCE

Career-Related Child Care Positions:

COUNSELOR, Racine Recreation Kids Camp, Racine, WI (1991-1992)
Led crafts, sports and field trips for a group of 10 children including several pre-schoolers.

NANNY, Private Child Care, Two Families, Bristol, WI (1990)
Assumed full responsibility summer-long for two 4 year olds and one 6 year old.

GYMNASTICS INSTRUCTOR, Frank's Fitness Club, Wind Point, WI (1989)
Led two one-hour children's classes daily, structuring activities appropriate to age and ability.

TEACHER AIDE, End of the Rainbow Day Care Center, Oak Creek, WI (1988-1989)
Provided nurturing care to 15-20 infants, toddlers and pre-schoolers, with TLC in abundance through holding, story-telling, song-leading and the like, and supervising meals and nap-times.

Other Part-Time and Summer Employment:

HOUSESITTING, Local Home, Pleasant Prairie, WI (1989-Present)
CASHIER, Sweet Treats Cafe, Kenosha, WI (1990-1991)
ASSISTANT MANAGER/SALES REP, Windham's, Milwaukee, WI (1988-1989)

EDUCATION

B.S., DEVELOPMENTAL PSYCHOLOGY, 1993. Marquette University, Milwaukee, WI

Studies applicable to Baccalaureate Degree:
Semester abroad, with extensive travels through Europe - Loyola Marymount, Rome, Italy

Student Leadership Activities: Sergeant at Arms; Judicial Board; Pledge Boards (Theta Phi Epsilon)
Community Service: in diverse social services; and heath care fund-raising campaigns.

GRADUATE, 1988. Kenosha High School. Achievement Award: Early Childhood Services.

Student Leadership Activities: Co-Captain, Varsity Gymnastics; Co-Captain, Varsity Track Team;
Accomplishments: Metropolitan League Champion, 100 Yd. Dash; State Track Finals, 1988.

AVA TAEGER

Telephone:
(406) 444-2537

177 Rolling Hills Drive
Helena, MT 59624

OBJECTIVE

CUSTOMER SERVICE

- Sensitivity to Needs, Wants and Concerns
- Fast Response Time • Creative Problem-Solving • Reliable Follow-Through

QUALIFIED BY

Specialized academic studies, and five years of related work experience in diverse business settings emphasizing heavy public contact and customer relations.

EDUCATION

BS, MANAGEMENT - In progress. 75% Completed. Montana State University, Bozeman, MT

Diploma, DATA PROCESSING, with honors, 1990. Computer Learning Institute, Missoula, MT

AREAS OF EFFECTIVENESS

- Human Relations
- Information and Referral
- Customer Tracking and Analysis
- Computerized Data Bases
- Administrative Support
- Financial and Managerial Accounting

EXPERIENCE

Part-Time Employment and Internships:

Interacted daily and extensively with all types of people - managers, clients, employers, deans, and students - in sometimes difficult or complex situations. Fielded questions and expedited service, building good will and stimulating new and continuing business.

ADMINISTRATIVE ASSISTANT, Montana State University, Bozeman, MT   (1991-Present)

- Served students in a business school placement office, as front-line resource person for program orientation, registration and use.

- Assisted employers from every sector of business in person and on the phone, taking job orders and supporting on-campus recruitment visits.

- Supported placement office staff with statistical data, graphic design, and screening and implementing requests for assistance.

- Keyed in, maintained and processed job information in HP 3000 computer.

ACCOUNTING/NEW ACCOUNTS ASSISTANT, Cascade Falls Bank, Alberton, MT (1989-1990)

- Reconciled bank accounts and maintained bank receipts; commended for error-free work.

- Interviewed bank customers for opening accounts; was nominated for loan officer training.

ASSISTANT TO THE BRANCH MANAGER, Green and Harper, Paradise, MT   (1988)

- Assisted in all financial management activities for a small business, including general bookkeeping, payroll, budget planning, coordination of monthly inventories, collection of accounts receivable and preparation of financial statements.

KEVIN KEEGAN

Telephone:
(617) 837-1429

90 Seacrest Road
Marshfield, MA 02050

OBJECTIVE

BROADCAST MEDIA
Entry Level Position with Growth Potential

Programming/News/Entertainment
• Research   • Editing   • Production   • On-Air Communications

QUALIFIED BY

Specialized professional studies and FCC licensing, and two years of hands-on media experience emphasizing the assessment, tracking and development of audience satisfaction. Creativity in generating and implementing ideas with high entertainment value, blended with practical judgment and good political instincts on appropriateness and timing of cutting edge material.

EDUCATION

B.A. ENGLISH/COMMUNICATIONS, BROADCASTING CONCENTRATION: 1992
Boston University, Boston, MA

Coursework related to Objective:

• Mass Media	• Advanced Radio Production	• Media Ethics	• Graphics
• Journalism	• Advanced Television Production	• Public Relations	• Drawing

KEY SKILLS

• Innovating   • Designing   • Planning   • Coordinating   • Presenting   • Human Relations

EXPERIENCE

Career-Related Contributed Services, Internship and Practicum:

MUSIC DIRECTOR/EXECUTIVE BOARD (1992); DISC JOCKEY (1990-1992)
NEWS EDITOR (1991); NEWSCASTER (1990). *WRJO*, Boston, MA
STAFF ARTIST/Editorial Cartoons, Ads, Drawings (1991-1992) *The Journal*, Boston, MA

• Created popular promos for a prime time music show, with audience requests for repeated play.

• Made weekly reports to *College Music Journal Magazine* of Top Ten Hard Rock Songs, incentivizing record companies to send new music by introducing selected cuts into play.

• Co-led fundraising campaigns to supplement budget of non-commercial station, building positive audience relations and generating income by super-deal compact disc sales.

• Recruited for key roles in news editing and music directing in recognition of proficiency.

• Handled all aspects of a bi-weekly broadcast of local and national news, including running the boards, and writing, editing and presenting of stories on-air.

Employment during College Studies:

ASST. MANAGER/PROJECTIONIST (1989-Present). United Cinemas, Hanover, MA
SALES ASSISTANT (1990-1992). Harbor View Video, Boston, MA

BERNARD KIRN

H: (208) 459-0616
O: (208) 377-8750

36 Magdalena Road
Caldwell, ID 83605

OBJECTIVE

PORTFOLIO MANAGEMENT - SECURITIES

QUALIFIED BY

- Eighteen years of diverse and increasingly responsible experience which included seven years as an in-house Financial Planner, and two years in corporate pension fund accounting.

- Active stock market investor for past 14 years with emphasis on growth stocks. Currently managing three portfolio accounts for other investors.

EXPERIENCE

Boise Cascade Corporation, Boise, Idaho

MANAGER EQUIPMENT LEASING	Management Information Systems	(1991-Present)
ACCOUNTING MANAGER	Management Information Systems	(1988-1990)
DIVISION ACCOUNTING MANAGER	Digital Systems Division	(1986-1988)
ACCOUNTING SUPERVISOR	Pension & Profit Sharing	(1983-1985)
FINANCIAL ANALYST	Corporate Profit Planning	(1982)
FINANCIAL & TAX ANALYST	Financial Planning Department	(1975-1981)

- Performed analytical studies on $50 million gain from stock liquidation - saved over $2 million for twenty clients by structuring financial plans, and participated in reinvestment decisions in securities, real estate and tax sheltered investments.

- Performed investment and tax analysis for clients on income properties valued at over $25 million, followed by profitable investments.

- Performed estate and trust planning for two estates valued at over $15 million; made decisions on restricted stock valuations and liquidations.

- Designed an on-line information system to allocate and monitor $20 million of annual personnel and computer resources to corporate divisions.

On Personal Investments:

- Researched, analyzed and invested in numerous small capitalized companies which have achieved high growth and earnings.

- Achieved an annual compounded rate of return comparable to S&P 500 rate of return for the last five years in a conservative account with an average of ten securities.

EDUCATION

MBA, FINANCE, 1974. University of Puget Sound, Tacoma, WA

BS, ECONOMICS, 1970. Fairfield University, Fairfield, CT

Prior coursework includes ten courses in Income Tax and Investments.

TONY RESTON

Telephone:
(401) 847-9762

44 Gately Road
Portsmouth, RI 02871

OBJECTIVE

FIELD SALES/GOLF PRODUCTS

- Positive Relationships with Pro Shops and Off-Course Retailers
- Favorable Product Positioning Strategies and Incentives
- Active Promotion of New and Existing Lines
- Strong Customer Service in Anticipating and Satisfying Needs

QUALIFIED BY

Avid personal enthusiasm for the game of golf over the past 12 years, with sustained involvement in tournament play;

Thorough familiarity with a broad range of golf apparel, shoes and equipment;

Success in stimulating donations to community organizations through sports fundraisers;

Demonstrated teamwork in co-management of a family business with up to $1M in annual sales through a marketing strategy based on quality, timeliness and reliability.

KEY SKILLS

Strategy

- Analyzing
- Planning
- Implementing
- Evaluating
- Fine-Tuning

Communications

- Listening
- Clarifying
- Recommending
- Motivating
- Assisting

AVOCATIONAL SPORTS INVOLVEMENT

- Named a Most Improved Player by *Golfer's World* in early stages of personal involvement with the game, lowering handicap from 34 to 17 within one year.

- Won championship of a major Club Trophy Tournament at home course in four ball match play.

- Solicited donations from local businesses to support youth athletics programs including a variety of raffle prizes in goods and services, and promoted participation in a benefit golf tournament at Glenwood Country Club by parents and friends of a local elementary school.

- Coached athletic programs for youth in two different competitive sports, instilling a commitment to excellence and sportsmanship. In soccer, this year's results: 21 wins/three ties in 24 games.

EXPERIENCE

VICE PRESIDENT/OWNER. Ace Products, Inc., Warwick, RI (1974-Present)
Packing materials manufacturer specializing in high durability industrial applications

Build and maintain solid relationships with a broad customer base, placing a premium on clear communication and high standards of performance in all phases of operations.

EDUCATION

B.A. Political Science, 1974. Providence College, Providence, RI

KIRK THAYER

Telephone:
(918) 661-0663

421 Graham Street
Bartlesville, OK 74004

OBJECTIVE

SALES REPRESENTATIVE/NUTRITIONAL PRODUCTS

QUALIFIED BY

Specialized business studies, and fourteen years of related professional experience in the health care industry evaluating and utilizing nutritional products for treatment of a diverse clientele, and sideline work experience emphasizing heavy public contact.

EDUCATION

MBA, HEALTH SERVICES MANAGEMENT, 1992. University of Tulsa, Tulsa, OK

BS, FOOD, NUTRITION AND DIETETICS, 1978. University of Wyoming, Laramie, WY

AREAS OF EFFECTIVENESS

COMMUNICATION

• Lectured on nutrition on behalf of Oklahoma Dietetic Association Speakers Bureau.

• Delivered presentations for the community as component of hospital public relations projects, including radio and television exposure, and meetings of 10-100 people.

• Lectured in symposia for healthcare professionals on normal and therapeutic nutritional care.

• Guided varied groups of tourists through Tulsa's historical sights and attractions.

MARKETING SUPPORT

• Developed marketing plan for an ambulatory care clinic; patient increase of 20% in 3 months.

• Performed cost/benefit analysis of a home total parenteral nutrition service.

NUTRITION

• Delivered nutritional care to hospitalized and ambulatory clients. Specialized in selection of proprietary formulas for enteral feeding.

• Stimulated enrollment of clients in public health nutrition programs, 3 out of every 5 contacted.

EXPERIENCE

Career-Related Employment:

CLINICAL DIETITIAN, Harmony Hospital, Claremore, OK	(1988-Present)
CLINICAL NUTRITIONIST, National Health Services, Muskogee, OK	(1985-1987)
HOME HEALTH DIETITIAN, Simmons Medical Clinic, Wagoner, OK	(1982-1985)
THERAPEUTIC DIETITIAN, Gregory Health Plan, Stillwater, OK	(1981-1982)
DIETITIAN, El Shalom Hospital, Jerusalem, Israel	(1979-1980)

Other Employment:

TOUR GUIDE/DRIVER, Abbott Tours & Travel, Tulsa, OK	(1990-Present)

MELANIE MALDEN

Telephone:
(617) 749-3402

4532 Washington Street
Hingham, MA 02043

OBJECTIVE

SALES/MARKETING - COMPUTERS

QUALIFIED BY

Specialized studies, and fifteen years of increasingly responsible professional experience with demonstrated leadership, planning, problem-solving, communication and promotional skills.

EDUCATION

Master of Business Administration Studies (in progress). Babson College, Wellesley, MA

Relevant Coursework:
- Marketing for Managers
- Counselor Selling
- Marketing Management
- Advertising Strategies
- Sales Development
- Managing Interpersonal Relations

Bachelor of Science and Master of Education, University of Massachusetts, Amherst, MA

AREAS OF EFFECTIVENESS

SALES & BUSINESS DEVELOPMENT

- Designed and implemented management level marketing training seminar. Developed marketing plans and promotional strategies for small business clients. Designed and conducted evaluations.

- Prospected local businesses to establish work experience sites and commitments to institute programs. Resulted in consistent job support and positive business-community relations.

- Wrote and developed successful grants; coordinated fund-raising efforts to institute new services sought by client and to expand existing program base.

MANAGEMENT

- Managed operational procedures at 8 sites including supervision and evaluation of 52 staff members. Controlled $1.1 million in budget/resource allocations.

- Negotiated program approval at local and state level to launch first-of-its-kind training project, expanding collaborative efforts of two large agencies as well as increasing training services.

- Administrator of computer-assisted adaptive technology classroom. Supervised computer system upgrade and installation process. Computer user/owner.

TRAINING

- Planned and conducted seminars for over 400 professionals at local/national conferences, improving agency exposure and increasing book sales revenue by 25%. Developed adult learner training materials to implement programs aimed at increasing productivity and motivation.

EXPERIENCE

Consultant, Malden & Associates, Hingham, MA	(1991-Present)
Principal, Suffolk County Office of Education, Boston, MA	(1984-Present)
Teacher, Suffolk County Superintendent of Schools, Boston, MA	(1979-1983)
Instructor/Consultant, Boston Public Schools, Boston, MA	(1978-1979)

MEMBERSHIP

American Marketing Association

CAROLINE KALE

Telephone:
(605) 996-4759

146 Miller Road
Mitchell, SD 57301

OBJECTIVE

MARKETING INTERNSHIP

QUALIFIED BY

Specialized professional studies, an internship in sales, work experience in diverse business settings, and student leadership positions using analytical, planning, organizing, communication and promotional skills to design and implement client-oriented services.

EDUCATION

MBA, MANAGEMENT - Completion: 1993. University of South Dakota, Vermillion, SD

BA, ECONOMICS, with honors, 1991. Augustana College, Sioux Falls, SD

Student Leadership Activities and Awards: Vice President, American Marketing Association Student Chapter; Award-Winning Community Service Officer; and Vice President of Sorority.

AREAS OF EFFECTIVENESS

PUBLICITY

Wrote over 50 press releases for newspapers and radio and television stations to stimulate awareness and build support for a range of student-sponsored community development projects. Media relations role also involved contacts with photographers and reporters for coverage of events.

FUND-RAISING

Coordinated six fund-raisers for the American Heart Association, including bike-a-thons, candy sales, and door-to-doors. Recruited and supervised volunteers of up to 100 people, and raised over $5,000.

COMMUNITY RELATIONS

Worked with medical personnel and public safety officers to establish campus-based CPR training, and enrolled over 75 students in the program.

Organized 50 students to assist in the logistics of three one-day blood drives for the community, coordinated publicity in flyers, posters and newspaper articles, and averaged 500 donors per event.

CUSTOMER RELATIONS

Served 500 customers per day in a fast-food restaurant, expediting orders and providing "service with a smile" to people of all ages and cultures. Won Employee of the Month Award for excellence in customer service performance.

Interviewed customers of a travel agency on the phone and in person and recommended packages tailored to their needs, as well as promoting special deals sponsored by the firm.

Served 200 customers per day in a pharmacy, suggesting items for purchase, filling orders, and resolving complaints, focusing on high quality service to stimulate buying and return business.

EXPERIENCE

Summer Work Experience during College Breaks:

Assistant Manager, McDonalds, Yankton, SD	(1992)
Sales Intern, Frontier Travel, Sioux Falls, SD	(1991)
Sales Clerk, Evergreen Pharmacy, Chester, SD	(1990)

HELEN KELLIHER

Telephone:
(801) 399-4931

4327 Hancock Street
Ogden, UT 84402

OBJECTIVE

ENTRY LEVEL POSITION/ADVERTISING

Product Promotion Strategies and Campaigns
• Positioning for Visibility • Building Profitability

QUALIFIED BY

Liberal arts degree honing skills in research, analysis, and writing, leadership positions in student government and competitive sports, and varied work experience in allied functions of marketing.

AREAS OF EFFECTIVENESS

- EVENT PLANNING
- PROMOTIONS
- MULTI-MEDIA PRESENTATIONS
- COPYWRITING AND EDITING
- CUSTOMER RELATIONS
- DIRECT SALES

RELATED ACCOMPLISHMENTS

For an under-construction 686,000 square foot office development:
- Arranged an introductory reception for 300 of Salt Lake City's top producing real estate brokers.
- Coordinated an appreciation day for 140 construction workers, including a full barbeque, souvenir t-shirts, and a drawing for dinners at select city restaurants.
- Developed script and photographic slides for a multi-media presentation showcasing the building.
- Contributed marketing strategy and design ideas for a bi-monthly promotional newsletter, including name, logo, issue themes, story topics, format, and graphics.
- Customized sale and leasing proposals to prospective tenants, and edited and proofed overall text.

Wrote feature articles, developed future topics, and assisted in layout, production and distribution of an 8-page monthly newsletter targeted to 200 employees of a major life insurance company.

Sold home furnishings for a specialty store with annual gross sales of $1M, maintaining positive customer relations with 150+ patrons daily.

EDUCATION

BA, ENGLISH, 1990. Brigham Young University, Provo, UT

Leadership Positions:
Award-Winning Public Speaker; Captain of Tennis Team; Community Council Representative

EXPERIENCE

Professional Positions:

CONTRACT ANALYST, Alta Health Strategies, Salt Lake City, UT	(1990-1991)
DIRECTOR, Summer Tennis Program, Logan Parks Department, Logan, UT	(1987-1988)

Additional Business Employment:

ADMINISTRATIVE SUPPORT, Ziona Bancorp, Salt Lake City, UT	(1992-Present)
SALES STAFF, Homes International, Willard, UT	(1989)

MEMBERSHIP

International Association of Business Communicators

VALERIE JANNELL

Telephone:
(908) 542-8696

56 Jamison Road
Eatontown, NJ 07724

OBJECTIVE

FINANCIAL PLANNING INTERNSHIP

- Tailoring Investments to Client Needs
- Optimizing Assets for Fiscal Growth
- Brokering Products for Profitability

QUALIFIED BY

Specialized graduate studies, and seven years of diversified business experience emphasizing skills in customer relations and salesmanship with an upscale clientele.

EDUCATION

MS, FINANCIAL PLANNING - In Progress. Rutgers University, New Brunswick, NJ

BS, FINANCE, 1985. Fordham University, Bronx, NY. Honors: Dean's List.

KEY SKILLS

- Analysis   - Planning   - Consultation   - Promotion   - Fiscal Management

RELATED ACCOMPLISHMENTS

Assisted several hundred customers per day with buying decisions, focusing on quality service, volume sales and return business for a specialty department store.

Interacted on a daily basis in the functional areas of personnel management, store merchandising and retail management for four designer boutiques.

Assisted in all financial management activities for a small business including general bookkeeping, payroll, budget planning, coordination of monthly inventories, collection of accounts receivables and preparation of financial statements.

Prepared federal and state tax forms for individuals and assisted in preparation of business tax returns as a volunteer income tax preparer.

Publicized internship programs through the use of lectures, slide presentations, posters and press releases. Recruited retail firms for a university career fair.

EXPERIENCE

ASSISTANT STORE MANAGER, Pierre LaCroix, Palm Beach, FL	(1990-1992)
SALESPERSON, Silk Creations, West Palm Beach, FL	(1988-1990)
PUBLICITY COORDINATOR, Cagney Retail Institute, NY, NY	(1986-1988)
MANAGEMENT TRAINING INTERN, Macy's, New Brunswick, NJ	(1985)

MEMBERSHIP

International Association for Financial Planning

CAREER-CHANGING

SHEILA REILLY

Telephone:
(312) 242-6194

3578 Parker Street
Aurora, IL 60507

OBJECTIVE

STAFF ACCOUNTANT/CPA FIRM

QUALIFIED BY

Specialized academic preparation at the graduate level, professional competence established by CPA examination, and diverse work experience emphasizing heavy public contact and practical judgment.

EDUCATION

MBA, ACCOUNTING, 1992. DePaul University, Chicago, IL

BA, PSYCHOLOGY, Northwestern University, Chicago, IL

Coursework Related to Career Objective:

- Financial Accounting
- Managerial & Cost Accounting
- Intermediate Accounting
- Business Law
- Multiple Proprietorships
- Advanced Accounting
- Auditing
- Accounting Theory/Research

KEY SKILLS

- Analysis   • Planning   • Problem-Solving   • Human Relations   • Adaptability

RELATED ACCOMPLISHMENTS

Passed the Practice, Business Law and Auditing sections of the uniform CPA examination on first attempt in May of 1992.

Supervised 30-50 employees of a university food service operation, overseeing all selection, training, scheduling, and direct service.

Planned, organized, and led a primary school open classroom with 8 learning centers, individualizing instruction and tracking performance of 20-40 students.

Served as a front-line representative with a heavy volume of customers of a public utility, trouble-shooting problems and expediting service.

Dealt with a broad cross-section of the public in the hospitality industry, relating to diverse personalities in service situations demanding tact, diplomacy, and humor.

Handled cash control and credit transactions of a retail service business averaging $15,000 weekly.

EXPERIENCE

Professional Employment:

Food Service Manager, Mundelein College, Chicago, IL	(1988-1989)
Instructor, Meridien School, Palatine, IL	(1979-1983)
Customer Service Representative, Ameritech, Chicago, IL	(1978-1979)

Other Employment:

Bartender, Marriott-Host International, Chicago, IL	(1989-Present)
Miscellaneous Food and Beverage Staff Positions, Evanston, IL	(1984-1987)

MEMBERSHIP

American Society of Woman Accountants

DELIA KENNEDY

Telephone:
(206) 455-1722

16 Iris Lane
Bellevue, WA 98008

OBJECTIVE

RISK MANAGEMENT SERVICES

• Loss Prevention   • Liability Reduction   • Insurance Analysis

QUALIFIED BY

Fourteen years of increasingly senior experience in the insurance industry, with significant responsibilities in handling claims for corporate accounts. Demonstrated strengths in cost containment strategies. Thoroughly grounded in hazard identification and risk reduction methods, as well as insurance company operations, coverage options, and settlement procedures.

KEY SKILLS

• Consulting • Investigating • Evaluating • Negotiating • Problem-Solving
• Risk Assessment • Loss History Analysis • Claims Management • Training and Development

RELATED ACCOMPLISHMENTS

• Supervised investigation, processing and settlement of complex claims of 100K plus, utilizing a network of legal, medical and financial advisors in making determinations, and consistently optimizing customer position under tight timeframes in a high volume environment.

• Provided consultation to corporate accounts on coverage adequacy and options in conjunction with claims processing activities for enhanced customer service.

• Conducted thorough analysis on the use of private investigators and their impact on cost containment objectives. Report was circulated throughout the company and drew accolades from members of top management.

• Currently serving as an arbitrator adjudicating intercompany disputes, assessing the merits of conflicting claims in reaching equitable, binding decisions.

• Conducted a series of seminars for technical staff on investigation and handling of cases involving serious personal injury and use of structured settlements as a settlement tool. Also, conducted well-received seminars for agents on claims procedures and coverage issues.

EXPERIENCE

Liberty Insurance Co., Bremerton, WA

CLAIM TECHNICAL SUPERVISOR   (1989-Present)

Monroe Insurance Co., Tacoma, WA

CLAIM TECHNICAL SUPERVISOR   (1989)
SENIOR CLAIM REPRESENTATIVE   (1984-1989)
FIELD CLAIMS REPRESENTATIVE   (1979-1984)

EDUCATION

BACHELOR OF SCIENCE, 1978. Lewis and Clark College, Portland, OR
ASSOCIATE IN CLAIMS. CPCU in Progress, 50% Completed. Insurance Institute of America

DENNIS HOLLAND

Telephone:
(615) 371-3267

33 Starr Lane
Brentwood, TN 37027

OBJECTIVE

TELECOMMUNICATIONS MANAGEMENT CONSULTING SERVICES

QUALIFIED BY

Specialized education, and over twenty years of experience in problem analysis, revenue and expense management and projections, consultation and public contact activities.

EDUCATION

MS, TELECOMMUNICATIONS MANAGEMENT, 1992
Tennessee State University, Nashville, TN

BS, BANKING AND FINANCE
Vanderbilt University, Nashville, TN

Coursework Relevant to Objective:

- Data Communications Systems
- Local Area Networks
- Network Design & Management
- Voice Networks & Communications
- Computers & Programming
- Financial & Managerial Accounting

KEY SKILLS

- Analysis & Problem-Solving
- Planning & Budgeting
- Contract Negotiation
- Customer Relations

RELATED ACCOMPLISHMENTS

In consultative services to large commercial accounts:

- Took over responsibility for a Marine Department with revenues of $100,000 and increased revenues to over $2M in five years, while maintaining profitability.

- Reviewed and analyzed problem accounts where losses were substantial. Devised and recommended loss prevention measures and means of greater assumption of risk by the insured.

- Represented some of the largest insurance companies in negotiating contracts with agents and brokers concerning the coverage of tugs and barges. Was authorized to commit resources of up to $5M on any one vessel.

EXPERIENCE

RISK MANAGEMENT CONSULTANT, Self-Employed, Belle Meade, TN   (1989-Present)

SR. UNDERWRITER, Provident Life & Accident Insurance, Chattanooga, TN   (1974-1989)

ACCOUNT EXECUTIVE, Ingram Industries, Nashville, TN   (1969-1973)

MEMBERSHIP

Society of Telecommunications Consultants

DEREK JARDIN

Telephone:
(402) 476-2051

542 Foley Street
Lincoln, NE 68508

OBJECTIVE

ADMINISTRATIVE MANAGEMENT

QUALIFIED BY

Over twenty years of varied managerial experience at all levels, up to and including executive management, plus extensive graduate business education. Special strengths in practical problem-solving, streamlining procedures, and expediting service within large, complex organizations.

AREAS OF EFFECTIVENESS

- Management Analysis
- Human Resources Management
- Training and Development
- Management Information Systems

- Organizational Effectiveness
- Operations Management
- Communications
- Quality Assurance

RELATED ACCOMPLISHMENTS

IN EXECUTIVE LEVEL MANAGEMENT:

- Initially, as the Special Assistant for Alternate Site Planning, surveyed a number of different locations for the establishment of a new branch of the Defense Language Institute. Identified, secured, remodelled and refurbished a 186,000 square foot facility to meet this need. Also selected and hired the 100 staff and faculty necessary for the operation.

  Served as the General Manager of this branch for the next three years, graduating over 2,000 students from the basic language courses while setting new records for low employee/student problems and high quality of the graduates. Annual budget was $4.6M.

IN SENIOR STAFF MANAGEMENT:

- As the Administrator of a US community in Germany, assisted the General Manager in supervising all support functions to include personnel management, logistics, and services, recreational activities and law enforcement with a workforce of 300 personnel supporting a population of 15,000.

- As the Assistant General Manager and Chief of Staff of a 600 person organization, directly supervised and coordinated all staff functions, and worked as planning officer, inspector and quality assurance consultant, and chief advisor to the General Manager.

- As a primary staff manager in a number of smaller organizations, supervised departments of operations, training and personnnel.

DEREK JARDIN   Page Two

IN MANAGEMENT CONSULTING:

- As Special Assistant to the Chief Executive Officer of a 20,000 person organization, performed management analyses in most of the staff functional areas to identify weaknesses and systemic malfunctions. Following performance problem analysis, developed and coordinated detailed remediation programs specifically tailored to optimize effectiveness and efficiency.

- Concurrently both in the US and abroad, also developed and implemented extensive Management by Objective programs and Information Systems focused on capturing key decision-making data and performance indicators of all subsidiary organizations.

EXPERIENCE

US ARMY OFFICER, up to the rank of Lieutenant Colonel   (1971-1992)

INSTRUCTOR, Ames Institute, Grand Island, NE   (1970-1971)

EDUCATION

MBA, INFORMATION SYSTEMS MANAGEMENT, 1992
Golden Gate University, San Francisco, CA

MBA, GENERAL MANAGEMENT, 1977
University of Maryland, College Park, MD

BA, PSYCHOLOGY, 1969
Creighton University, Omaha, NE

30 months of Army Schools. Coursework applicable to career objective:

- Government Contracting
- Personnel Management
- Project Planning
- Labor Relations
- Program Budget Management
- Equal Employment Opportunity
- Time and Resource Management
- Organizational Leadership
- Assorted Computer Courses
- Organizational Effectiveness

MEMBERSHIPS

- American Management Association   • Administrative Management Society

• Institute of Management Consultants

DENISE PARADI

Telephone:
(603) 883-5998

264 Bellingham Road
Nashua, NH 03060

OBJECTIVE

PARALEGAL SUPPORT SERVICES

• Responsiveness to Direction   • Fast and Accurate Production   • Reliable Follow-Through

QUALIFIED BY

Paraprofessional studies in legal language, procedures and resources, supported by seven years of experience emphasizing an ability to juggle multiple responsibilities, meet deadlines, and handle sensitive matters with tact and discretion.

EDUCATION

BS, PARALEGAL STUDIES - In Progress. Notre Dame College, Manchester, NH
Completed Coursework:
• Introduction to Paralegal   • US Judicial Systems   • Business Law   • Corporate Law

AA, 1985. Bunker Hill Community College, Boston, MA

KEY SKILLS

• Communication • Organizing • Problem-Solving • Expediting • Tracking • Documentation
Technical Proficiencies:
• Software: Multimate and Wang Word Processing; Lotus 1-2-3
• Computers: IBM PC and Compatibles
• Office: Dictaphone, Xerox, Facsimile, Calculators

RELATED ACCOMPLISHMENTS

For a savings institution loan servicing department:
• Processed commercial and residential loan documents associated with foreclosure and bankruptcy proceedings, including promissory notes, mortgages and riders, loan applications, guarantors, and appraisals.
• Communicated with delinquent borrowers regarding payment arrangements, and issue demands for payment as needed while strictly observing collection law boundaries.
• Tracked return and sale dates on foreclosures, and check and complete filings for relief from stays.
• Notified attorneys regarding delinquent status of post-petition payments.
• Assisted customers with a wide variety of servicing problems, providing information and referrals in a timely fashion.

For non-profit mental health organizations offering a wide spectrum of services, provided support including: fielding of 50+ phone calls per day; word processing; recordkeeping; and purchasing.

In both individual contributor and managerial roles, contributed to client-centered services through clear communications, efficient administration of daily operations, and detailed reporting.

EXPERIENCE

COLLECTION REPRESENTATIVE, First New Hampshire Banks, Nashua, NH   (1990-Present)
PROGRAM MANAGER, Center for Retarded Citizens, Manchester, NH   (1988-1990)
SUPERVISOR/CASE WORKER, Family Support Services, Derry, NH   (1986-1988)

DIANE FLEMING

Telephone:
(803) 833-4485

532 Aviary Road
Clinton, SC 29325

OBJECTIVE

HUMAN RESOURCES/EMPLOYMENT SERVICES

- Close Collaboration with Line Managers in Identifying Staffing Needs
- Active Sourcing of Qualified Candidates
- Applicant Pool Prescreening and Interviewing

QUALIFIED BY

Specialized professional studies, and extensive and varied liaison experience in business implementing management objectives and exercising practical judgment.

EDUCATION

MBA, 1992. BS, MANAGEMENT, 1989. Clemson University, Clemson, SC

Coursework Relevant to Objective:

- Human Resources Management
- Managerial Analysis & Communication
- Policy Formulation & Administration

- Psychology of the Interview
- Human Problems of Administration
- Human Relations

KEY SKILLS

In internal communications with management, professional and support employees, and external communications with customers and vendors:

- Assessing Needs
- Identifying Resources
- Developing Strategies

- Administering Programs
- Solving Problems
- Negotiating Agreements

RELATED ACCOMPLISHMENTS

For a corporation in a service industry:

- Worked closely with management on planning and implementation of an accounts receivable system that increased monthly collections by 25%.

- Interviewed department supervisors, then designed and implemented a credit card control system which stopped the fraudulent use of funds.

- Consulted with subsidiaries in performance problem analysis, and developed and coordinated detailed programs to promote efficiency.

- Acted as a liaison between management and employees, advising and counseling to maintain productivity while going through a difficult merger.

- Communicated with a broad cross-section of the public, relating to payment of accounts in situations demanding judgment and tact. Also promoted and negotiated special discount plans.

EXPERIENCE

ACCOUNTANT, Policy Management Systems, Columbia, SC   (1972-Present)
PERSONNEL REPRESENTATIVE, Piedmont Industries, Inc., Greenville, SC   (1971-1972)

MEMBERSHIP

Society for Human Resource Management

AND NOW—

Different Objectives/Different Resumes for the Same Person . . .

The following resumes dramatically illustrate how feasible it is to tailor your experience to varied kinds of career opportunities. They reflect a strategic approach to resume development very clearly and compellingly through a series of examples of two or more distinctly different resumes developed for each individual.

While varying greatly in career stage, career focus, level of responsibility and the like, each of the people featured in the next section decided to look for different kinds of work concurrently. In all cases, for a variety of reasons, it was desirable to explore employment possibilities in more than one area of specialization.

A biographical resume—get the history down and let it speak for itself—is a temptingly easy approach to developing a general, all-purpose resume. This resume style chronicles educational and work experiences in as clear and impressive a manner as possible.

In line with strategic resume development principles, though, these people chose a more rigorous, conceptually demanding approach, powerfully persuasive in impact. They went the extra mile in making sure that their ''Plan B'' was supported by a separate and distinct second resume, as carefully crafted as the resume for their first area of preference. The objective of each resume was to define the type of work sought, which led to distinctly different formulations of experience to address the target audience.

Relevance—The Key to Effectiveness

It is this tailoring of personal skills and experiences to support a particular career focus that is the hallmark of strategic resume development. It shows understanding of the hiring concerns of prospective employers and an attunement to the classical marketing principle of linking what you have to what the customer wants.

With an awareness of marketplace needs, a sense of your transferable skills and some creative wordsmithing, you can very effectively influence how people see you in regard to their enterprises. And whether you choose to pursue one major path of opportunity or two or more possible areas, may the following resumes remind you of your freedom to structure your written communications about yourself creatively and persuasively for what you most want to do.

MOLLY CORBETT

Telephone:
(617) 545-1271

22 Avon Road
Scituate, MA 02066

OBJECTIVE

TRAVEL AND TOURISM MARKETING SUPPORT

- For Work, Study and Leisure Abroad -
Program Design, Development, Promotion, and Coordination

- Contributing Roles -
• Trip & Meeting Planning • Promotional Materials Writing • Travelers' Guide & Friendly Service

QUALIFIED BY

• Extensive independent and group travel abroad, and strength in two foreign languages;
• Intensive college training polishing language arts skills to a high degree; and
• Work experience emphasizing customer service, organization, and timely follow-through.

AREAS OF EFFECTIVENESS

Creative Concepts, Ideas and Theme-Building

Logistical Arrangements, Trouble-Shooting and Problem-Solving

Production Skills:
Use of 35 Millimeter Camera for Portrait, Action and Environmental Shots
Use of Word Processing Systems - NBI 300 and 6400, and Xerox 860

Foreign Languages:
Working Knowledge of French and Spanish; German Studies in Progress

PERSONAL TRAVELS

• Air, rail and motor trips through the USA and Canada;
• Three trips, from 6-12 weeks each, through 18 European countries;
• Skilled in itinerary planning, maximizing travel budget, sourcing off-the-beaten-track attractions, noting customs of interest, and moving and connecting with ease and enthusiasm in new cultures.

EDUCATION

MFA, ENGLISH LITERATURE/ CREATIVE WRITING, 1992. Simmons College, Boston, MA

BA, ENGLISH LITERATURE, with honors, 1987. Emmanuel College, Boston, MA

Literary Criticism Summer Writing Program, 1991. Oxford University, Oxford, England

EXPERIENCE

Administrative Support Positions Financing College and Graduate Studies:

Peter Bates, Esq., Hanover, MA	(1990-Present)
Noble & Reston, Hingham, MA	(1987-1990)
Sullivan Sports Co., Quincy, MA	(1984-1986)

Writing Affiliations:

Promotional Writer - WGBH TV Channel 2 Auction, 1992. Boston, MA
Member, International Association of Business Communications

MOLLY CORBETT

Telephone:
(617) 545-1271

22 Avon Road
Scituate, MA 02066

OBJECTIVE

WRITER/EDITOR: BUSINESS COMMUNICATIONS

Clear, concise and creative writing in support of single or multiple corporate needs, including:

- Employee Newsletters   • Marketing Materials   • Training Guides

QUALIFIED BY

Intensive training in writing on the undergraduate and graduate levels, polishing language arts to a high degree in the development of concepts, delineation of themes, and transmission of ideas and information to targeted audiences.

WRITING STRENGTHS

- Wide Vocabulary and Accurate Spelling
- Clear Sentence Structure
- Correct Syntax, Grammar and Punctuation
- Simplicity in Style

Business Writing Sample Portfolio upon Request, Featuring:

- Interviews with Executives   • Company and Employee News Stories   • Feature Stories
- Press Releases • Ads • How-To Guides • Business Letters • Memoranda • Forms

ASSOCIATED SKILLS

- Photography: Use of 35 Millimeter Camera, with Standard, Zoom and Wide Angle Lenses Portrait, Action, and Environmental Shots

- Word Processing: Use of NBI 300 and 6400, and Xerox 860 Systems

EDUCATION

MFA, ENGLISH LITERATURE/ CREATIVE WRITING, 1992. Simmons College, Boston, MA

BA, ENGLISH LITERATURE, with honors, 1987. Emmanuel College, Boston, MA

Literary Criticism Summer Writing Program, 1991. Oxford University, Oxford, England

EXPERIENCE

Administrative Support Positions Financing College and Graduate Studies:

Peter Bates, Esq., Hanover, MA	(1990-Present)
Noble & Reston, Hingham, MA	(1987-1990)
Sullivan Sports Co., Quincy, MA	(1984-1986)

Related Accomplishments:
- Extensive proofreading, editing, and memo and correspondence drafting experience; and
- Heavy client contact, establishing rapport, drawing out concerns, and expediting service.

Writing Affiliations:

Promotional Writer - WGBH TV Channel 2 Auction, 1992. Boston, MA
Member, International Association of Business Communications

JESSE HANIFY

Home: (216) 425-9536
Messages: (216) 425-8742

392 Shipley Road
Twinsburg, OH 44087

OBJECTIVE

SECONDARY SCHOOL TEACHING/GRADES 7-12

• Innovative Approaches to Teaching and Learning • Positive Reinforcement for Peak Performance

QUALIFIED BY

Specialized professional studies and certification, eight years of substitute teaching requiring quick adapting to new and varied situations, and extensive involvement in youth community programs. Dedicated to helping students become all that they can be, developing self-esteem and confidence along with academic strengths. Versatility, adaptability and enthusiasm.

EDUCATION

B.S. EDUCATION, 1973. Ohio Wesleyan University, Delaware, OH
Member, Phi Alpha Theta, History Honor Society
Social Studies Secondary School Credential, State of Ohio

KEY SKILLS

• Curriculum Development
• Instructional Strategies and Methods

• Classroom Management
• Extracurricular Program Delivery

RELATED ACCOMPLISHMENTS

• Taught varied subjects in an inner city elementary school with a multi-cultural student body, working with normal, slow learner and autistic children on mastery of basic skills. Effectiveness has led to repeated and frequent requests to take on new assignments.

• Gained frequent assignments over several years in every middle school and high school of a large urban school district, teaching in college preparatory, business, and voc/tech areas.

• Established an intermural basketball league of middle schools from several suburban towns, recruiting referees, arranging logistics of transportation, uniforms, practice and game schedules, and awards ceremonies. Served as coach to championship-winning team for four successive years, with excellence in play, sportsmanship and teamwork as key operating values.

• Planned and facilitated classes, workshops and weekends away for high school students, focusing on self-awareness, personal growth, wellness and service to the community.

EXPERIENCE

Substitute Assignments:
TEACHER, Alden Marlin School, Cleveland, OH   (1992-Present)
TEACHER, Akron Public Schools, Akron, OH   (1974-1981)

Contributed Services:
TEACHER, CCD, Grace Church, Summit, OH   (1971-1975; 1992-Present)
COACH & ATHLETIC DIRECTOR, Mission School, Summit, OH   (1971-1975)

Business Sector Employment:
Sr. Tape Librarian, Network Technician, and Sr. Computer Operator
     Ameritrust Corp., Cleveland, OH   (1981-1991)
Computer Operator, Metropolitan Services, Youngstown, OH   (1973-1981)

JESSE HANIFY

Home: (216) 425-9536
Messages: (216) 425-8742

392 Shipley Road
Twinsburg, OH 44087

OBJECTIVE

PRODUCT SUPPORT/CUSTOMER SERVICE

- Assistance in Selection and Use of Appropriate Products and Services
- Resolution of Order Fulfillment Problems
- Initiative to Anticipate Needs and Give "Service Plus"

QUALIFIED BY

Over a decade of business experience focusing on the building and maintenance of a high level of satisfaction on the part of both internal and external customers by fast turn-around time, effective coordination of resources, and dependable follow-through. Specialized studies, work experience and community service in education emphasizing a dedicated personal commitment and high level of professionalism brought to helping relationships. Attentiveness, patience and enthusiasm.

KEY SKILLS

- Listening/Clarifying • Investigating/Tracking • Trouble-Shooting/Problem-Solving
- Orienting • Advising • Coaching • Training

RELATED ACCOMPLISHMENTS

Proven ability to communicate with a wide range of people with various needs, successfully interacting with executives, information systems professionals, vendors and non-technical users:

- Monitored and controlled the automated teller network consisting of 400 locations statewide for a major regional bank. Handled problem resolution calls from over 2,500 users and maintained up time of 90%.
- Maintained Customer Information Control System for the entire corporation with 99% up time.

Adapted to new and changing conditions on a constant basis as a substitute teacher in two school districts, establishing rapport and facilitating learning with diverse student groups.

Founded an intermural basketball league for youth, and served as coach to championship-winning team for four successive years, with excellence in play, sportsmanship and teamwork as key operating values. As well, planned and facilitated classes, workshops and weekends away for high school students focusing on self-awareness, personal growth and service to the community.

EDUCATION

B.S. EDUCATION, 1973, with honors. Ohio Wesleyan University, Delaware, OH

EXPERIENCE

Technical Support Services:

SR. TAPE LIBRARIAN, NETWORK TECHNICIAN, & SR. COMPUTER OPERATOR
    Ameritrust Corp., Cleveland, OH   (1981-1991)
COMPUTER OPERATOR, Metropolitan Services, Youngstown, OH   (1973-1981)

Non-Technical Support Services:

SUBSTITUTE TEACHER
    Alden Marlin School, Cleveland, OH (1991-Present) and Akron Public Schools (1974-1981)
CONTRIBUTED SERVICES IN TEACHING AND COACHING
    Grace Church and Mission School, Summit, OH   (1992-Present; 1971-1975)

JOAN BUCKLEY

Telephone:
(505) 827-6200

1270 Desert Hills Rd.
Santa Fe, NM 87503

OBJECTIVE

TECHNICAL TRAINING/HR SOFTWARE PACKAGES

• Internal Support Services to Managers and Staff
• Orientation and Coaching on Program Features, Benefits and Methods

QUALIFIED BY

Two years of direct experience in assisting users in mastery and effective utilization of personnel and payroll applications and nine years of in-house corporate experience overseeing HR and accounting functions, backed by specialized degree and extensive continuing education.

Demonstrated strength in managing multiple demands in time-pressured conditions, with fast response and reliable follow-through on problem resolution. Ability to communicate complex subject matter in clear and simple terms. Calm, patient and supportive personal manner.

KEY SKILLS

• Consultation • Needs Assessment • Advising • Instructing • Assisting

EXPERIENCE

Software Solutions, Santa Fe, NM
A developer/vendor of specialized business applications

CUSTOMER SERVICE MANAGER (1991-Present)

• Interact with over 200 clients in phone communications, averaging 40 calls a day for quick and in-depth trouble-shooting on software questions.

• Conduct intensive training programs for applications users, providing step-by-step multi-media instruction and guided practice. Evaluations consistently commend clarity, humor and openness.

Rogers Development Corp., Albuquerque, NM
A multi-division real estate development company with over 6,000 employees

DIRECTOR OF PERSONNEL (1989-1990) Condominium Division
PERSONNEL MANAGER (1988-1989); HR GENERALIST (1985-1987) Headquarters Division

• Handled all aspects of personnel administration in increasingly responsible positions, including recruitment, selection, compensation, benefits, employee relations, training and development.

• Assisted in implementation of Software Solutions personnel and payroll computer systems, working closely with MIS Department and line and staff managers to clarify concerns, determine needs and ensure a speedy, trouble-free automation process.

A/R SUPERVISOR (1983-1985); ASST. A/R SUPERVISOR (1981-1983) Residential Division

• Supervised a staff of six employees in tracking and collecting rent from 6,000 residential units and two television stations, while maintaining positive customer relations. Contributed to the design and implementation of an A/R program for an IBM System 38 computer.

EDUCATION

B.S., HUMAN RESOURCES, 1987. University of New Mexico, Albuquerque, NM

JOAN BUCKLEY

Telephone:
(505) 827-6200

1270 Desert Hills Rd.
Santa Fe, NM 87503

OBJECTIVE

EMPLOYMENT COUNSELOR

• High Quality Reemployment Support Services   • Public and Private Sector Partnership-Building

QUALIFIED BY

Thorough understanding of recruitment and selection practices and benefit programs
through five years of increasingly responsible experience in human resources positions.

Extensive experience in counseling and advising people of varied occupational specialties
and levels of responsibility on job transition and career development issues.

Demonstrated strength in managing multiple demands in time-pressured conditions, with fast
response and reliable follow-through on problem resolution. Ability to communicate complex
subject matter in clear and simple terms. Calm, patient and supportive personal manner.

KEY SKILLS

• Consultation • Needs Assessment • Advising • Assisting • Coordinating • Presentations

RELATED ACCOMPLISHMENTS

Handled all aspects of personnel administration for a multi-division real estate development
company with over 6,000 employees:

• Oversaw the employment function for professional and support staff in all respects, including
  definition of hiring needs and selection criteria with managers, utilization of placement services
  and advertising to source a qualified applicant pool, conducting pre-screening interviews, and
  serving as point of contact with prospective recruits.

• Provided counseling and advice on a regular basis to employees across the board on work
  satisfaction and effectiveness, and in particular to those affected by down-sizing or other job-
  related crises. Assisted in developing practical action plans for career recovery and growth.

• Advised departing employees of rights and benefits relevant to government programs and services
  in health insurance continuation programs and unemployment coverage.

• Played key liaison role between Human Resources and line and staff managers, clarifying
  concerns and determining needs in numerous matters relating to staffing and implementation
  of automated Human Resource information systems.

EXPERIENCE

Directly Related Experience:

DIRECTOR OF PERSONNEL (1989-1990) Condominium Division
PERSONNEL MANAGER (1988-1989); HR GENERALIST (1985-1987) Headquarters Division
Rogers Development Corp., Albuquerque, NM

Other Business Experience:

CUSTOMER SERVICE MANAGER, Software Solutions, Santa Fe, NM (1991-Present)
A/R SUPERVISORY POSITIONS, Rogers Development Corp., Albuquerque, NM (1981-1985)

EDUCATION

B.S., HUMAN RESOURCES, 1987. University of New Mexico, Albuquerque, NM

SONNY PETRAS

Telephone:
(404) 933-2984

336 Fairmont Street
Marietta, GA 30067

OBJECTIVE

MANAGEMENT POSITION/UNIVERSITY ADMISSIONS AND RECORDS

- Systems and Procedures for Timely Processing of Applications
- Collaborative Relationships with Faculty
- Service-Oriented Dealings with Prospective and Current Students and Alumni

QUALIFIED BY

Four years of direct experience in university admissions and records using planning, decision-making, problem-solving and communication skills to assess applicants, stimulate enrollments, and coordinate and streamline associated support services. Diversified promotional and administrative experience in higher education and the business world.

EXPERIENCE

ADMISSIONS OFFICER, Emory University, Atlanta, GA   (1989-Present)

- Managed processing of over 5,000 applications per year including high school and community college scholarship applicants and undergraduate and international admissions.

- Counseled prospective and current students on academic matters, presented petitions to deans and committees on admissions, conveyed decisions, and assisted in educational planning.

- Assisted in the automation of admissions department, contributing to systems analysis and design to maximize time and expedite a decision-making process directly tied to enrollment revenues.

- Maintained and updated the undergraduate admissions policy manual; gathered information on the educational systems of more than eighty countries.

DIRECTOR OF ALUMNI AFFAIRS, Executive Development Center, Marietta, GA   (1984-1986)

- Planned and organized fund-raising drives and events, soliciting contributions from alumni, industry and foundations, with annual proceeds of $400,000.

- Administered all facets of management and executive development seminar programs. Scheduled events, sourced facilities and negotiated favorable terms, and coordinated transportation, lodging and training programs. Annual institutional profit: $300,000.

Previous employment as: Sales Manager, Sales Representative and Administrative Analyst.

EDUCATION

MBA, ACCOUNTING, 1992;   CERTIFICATE, INFORMATION SCIENCE, 1988
Emory University, Atlanta, GA

BA, COMMUNICATIONS, 1979
Loyola University, New Orleans, LA

MEMBERSHIPS

American Association of Collegiate Registrars and Admissions Officers
National Association for Foreign Student Affairs

SONNY PETRAS

Telephone:
(404) 933-2984

336 Fairmont Street
Marietta, GA 300678

OBJECTIVE

AUDITING POSITION/CPA FIRM

QUALIFIED BY

Multi-disciplinary studies, bookkeeping for an upscale retail store, and twelve years of diversified administrative and promotional experience using analytical, trouble-shooting and interpersonal skills to assure efficient and profitable operations.

EDUCATION

MBA, ACCOUNTING, 1992. Emory University, Atlanta, GA

CERTIFICATE, INFORMATION SCIENCE, 1988. Emory University, Atlanta, GA

BA, COMMUNICATIONS, 1979. Loyola University, New Orleans, LA

AREAS OF EFFECTIVENESS

FINANCIAL RECORDS AND REPORTS

• Managed bookkeeping function for a retail store with annual sales of $500,000.

• Assisted in preparation of financial and operational reports for a major bank.

COMPUTER SYSTEMS AND OPERATIONS

• Assisted in the automation of a university admissions department, contributing to systems analysis and design to maximize time and expedite decision-making process directly tied to revenues.

• Oversaw all facets of a computer training facility, including scheduling, demonstration of HP 3000 computers, development of back-up systems in case of system failure, interface with outside technicians for maintenance and repair of hardware, and tutoring of trainees.

SALES AND BUSINESS DEVELOPMENT

• Directed sales and marketing activities for a specialty store of high-end men's clothing, targeting a core group and broader base of regular customers, and walk-in trade.

• Sold 35 condominiums in high rise towers for a real estate developer, ranging in price from $70,000-$200,000.

• Managed processing of over 5,000 applications per year including high school and community college scholarship applicants and undergraduate and graduate admissions. Subsequent annual tuition payments averaged $6,500 per person.

• Administered all facets of management and executive development seminar programs. Scheduled events, sourced facilities and negotiated favorable terms, and coordinated transportation, lodging and training programs. Annual institutional profit: $300,000.

EXPERIENCE

ADMISSIONS OFFICER, Emory University, Atlanta, GA   (1989-Present)
SALES MANAGER, Classic Styles, Fair Oaks, GA   (1986-1988)
DIRECTOR OF ALUMNI AFFAIRS, Executive Development Center, Marietta, GA (1984-1986)
SALES REPRESENTATIVE, Johnson Construction, Inc., So. Decatur, GA   (1981-1983)
ADMINISTRATIVE ANALYST, Fidelity Bank & Trust Co., Atlanta, GA   (1981)

MEMBERSHIP

National Society of Public Accountants: Student Chapter

RITA STERLING

Telephone:
(415) 493-7169

42 Winslow Road
Palo Alto, CA 94304

OBJECTIVE

DATA PROCESSING INFORMATION CENTER

- Technical Writing   • Employee Training

Corporate Services to Build Job Effectiveness and Enhance Productivity in the Use of Computers.

QUALIFIED BY

- Extensive data processing coursework, with practical emphasis on programming design and structure in several computer languages.
- Twenty plus years of applicable experience in foreign language instruction and program management emphasizing the development of detailed individualized learning guides and provision of tutorial and group instruction.

KEY SKILLS

- Performance Problem, Task and Goal Analysis
- Course Design
- Materials Development

- Instructional Strategies and Methods
- Seminar Leadership
- Personal Coaching

RELATED ACCOMPLISHMENTS

DIRECTLY QUALIFYING EXPERIENCE -

Computer Languages: C, C++, ADA, COBOL, Pascal, and Assembly; IBM PC

Varied exercises in programming techniques for business applications:

As part of coursework, wrote modular program systems that get, store and process data, and report results.Emphasized record and file organization, design, and maintenance with error traps. Utilized table processing, searches, sorts, character string processing, stacks, linked lists, on-line input, and data files.

Programs for personal financial management and professional effectiveness:

Own and utilize an IBM-XT for personal programming and word processing projects, including amortization tables, and work-related tracking systems for attendance and performance data.

APPLICABLE NON-TECHNICAL EXPERIENCE -

On the Job:

Planned, designed, wrote and implemented an individualized, self-guided and self-paced instructional program for learning Spanish in a public secondary school classroom. As well, provided traditional classroom instruction to groups ranging in size from 12-40 students

Performed a broad range of management functions as foreign language department chairperson for 20 years, including department goal, objective, and standard setting, systems and procedure development, work planning and simplification, budgeting and cost control, purchasing and inventory control, and master scheduling.

Avocationally:

Conducted intensive interviews with 25-20 candidates per year for the past 11 years for college admissions, asking probing and clarifying questions to define attributes recommending selection.

RITA STERLING   Page Two

EDUCATION

M.Ed. University of California, Berkeley, CA

BA, with Honors. Smith College, Northampton, MA

Non-technical professional development seminars relevant to career objective:

Individualized Learning; Accounting Procedures
Golden Gate University, San Francisco, CA

Specialized Programming Studies:

Twelve courses, including basic and advanced instruction in six computer languages. GPA: 3.75
DeAnza College, Cupertino, CA

EXPERIENCE

Professional Employment:

FOREIGN LANGUAGE DEPARTMENT CHAIRPERSON   (1973-1993)

SECONDARY SCHOOL SPANISH TEACHER   (1970-1993)

Fremont High School, Fremont, CA

Contributed Services:

INTERVIEWER   (1978-Present)

Smith Schools Committee, Bay Area

TRIP LEADER   (1975-Present)

Expeditions Unlimited, San Francisco, CA

MEMBERSHIPS

Society for Technical Communication

Association for Women in Computing

RITA STERLING

Telephone:
(415) 493-7169

42 Winslow Road
Palo Alto, CA 94304

OBJECTIVE

ENTRY LEVEL COMPUTER PROGRAMMING

QUALIFIED BY

- Extensive data processing coursework with hands-on, practical emphasis on programming design and structure in several computer languages.

- Twenty plus years of applicable experience in foreign language instruction and program management emphasizing precise use of syntax and grammar and structured support for task effectiveness through detailed individualized learning programs.

KEY SKILLS

In Design and Maintenance of Both Computer and Foreign Language Programs, Experienced in:

- Analyzing and Classifying Data;
- Defining Desired End Products and Anticipating Needs;
- Developing Step-by-Step Plans and Writing Instructions
- Checking and Rechecking for Error; and
- Refining, Streamlining and Testing for Efficiency and Effectiveness.

RELATED ACCOMPLISHMENTS

DIRECTLY QUALIFYING EXPERIENCE -

Computer Languages: C, C++, ADA, COBOL, Pascal, and Assembly; IBM PC

Varied exercises in programming techniques for business applications:

As part of coursework, wrote modular program systems that get, store and process data, and report results.Emphasized record and file organization, design, and maintenance with error traps. Utilized table processing, searches, sorts, character string processing, stacks, linked lists, on-line input, and data files.

Programs for personal financial management and professional effectiveness:

Own and utilize an IBM-XT for personal programming and word processing projects, including amortization tables, and work-related tracking systems for attendance and performance data.

APPLICABLE NON-TECHNICAL EXPERIENCE -

On the Job:

Planned, designed, wrote and implemented an individualized, self-guided and self-paced instructional program for learning Spanish in a public secondary school classroom. As well, provided traditional classroom instruction to groups ranging in size from 12-40 students

Performed a broad range of management functions as foreign language department chairperson for 20 years, including department goal, objective, and standard setting, systems and procedure development, work planning and simplification, budgeting and cost control, purchasing and inventory control, and master scheduling.

Avocationally:

Conducted intensive interviews with 25-20 candidates per year for the past 11 years for college admissions, asking probing and clarifying questions to define attributes recommending selection.

RITA STERLING

EDUCATION

M.Ed. University of California, Berkeley, CA

BA, with Honors. Smith College, Northampton, MA

Non-technical professional development seminars relevant to career objective:

Individualized Learning; Accounting Procedures
Golden Gate University, San Francisco, CA

Specialized Programming Studies:

Twelve courses, including basic and advanced instruction in six computer languages. GPA: 3.75
DeAnza College, Cupertino, CA

EXPERIENCE

Professional Employment:

FOREIGN LANGUAGE DEPARTMENT CHAIRPERSON   (1973-1993)

SECONDARY SCHOOL SPANISH TEACHER   (1970-1993)

Fremont High School, Fremont, CA

Contributed Services:

INTERVIEWER   (1978-Present)

Smith Schools Committee, Bay Area

TRIP LEADER   (1975-Present)

Expeditions Unlimited, San Francisco, CA

MEMBERSHIPS

Society for Technical Communication

Association for Women in Computing

NOTES

FOR OTHER FIFTY-MINUTE SELF-STUDY BOOKS
SEE THE BACK OF THIS BOOK.

FOR OTHER FIFTY-MINUTE SELF-STUDY BOOKS
SEE THE BACK OF THIS BOOK.

NOTES

FOR OTHER FIFTY-MINUTE SELF-STUDY BOOKS
SEE THE BACK OF THIS BOOK.

NOTES

FOR OTHER FIFTY-MINUTE SELF-STUDY BOOKS
SEE THE BACK OF THIS BOOK.

NOTES

FOR OTHER FIFTY-MINUTE SELF-STUDY BOOKS
SEE THE BACK OF THIS BOOK.

NOTES

We hope you enjoyed this book. If so, we have good news for you. This title is part of the best-selling *FIFTY-MINUTE*™ *Series* of books. All *Series* books are similar in size and identical in price. Several are supported with training videos (identified by the symbol **Ⓥ** next to the title).

FIFTY-MINUTE Books and Videos are available from your distributor. A free catalog is available upon request from Crisp Publications, Inc., 1200 Hamilton Court, Menlo Park, California 94025.

FIFTY-MINUTE Series Books & Videos organized by general subject area.

Management Training:

Management Training (continued):

Personal Improvement:

Human Resources & Wellness:

Human Resources & Wellness (continued):

Communications & Creativity:

Customer Service/Sales Training:

Small Business & Financial Planning:

Adult Literacy & Learning:

Career/Retirement & Life Planning:

TO ORDER BOOKS OR VIDEOS FROM THE FIFTY-MINUTE SERIES, PLEASE CONTACT YOUR LOCAL DISTRIBUTOR OR CALL 1-800-442-7477 TO FIND A DISTRIBUTOR IN YOUR AREA.